Television Killed Advertising
by Paul Ashby

Edited by Edward Keating

Paul Ashby pioneered interactive marketing communication 25 years ago. He has written and produced interactive events in Australia, Japan, Singapore, USA and the UK. He wrote and produced the world's first regularly scheduled interactive television show, "Su opinion est muy importante" (Your opinion is very important) broadcast on Channel 7, Manila, Philippines, sponsored by Proctor & Gamble.

He is interested in reading, travel, photography, music (especially jazz) and movies. Currently residing in Somerset, England, having also lived and worked in Sydney, Australia, Los Angeles, USA and Johannesburg, South Africa.

Would you like to discover the incredible results to be attained by using interactive communication?

Paul is currently offering his techniques as a partner in Renaissance Marketing, based in the UK.

To read more of Paul's thoughts on the advertising industry, check out his blog at: http://interactivetelevisionorinteractivetv.blogspot.com

Or, to contact Paul direct, email him at: paul@renaissancemarketing.co.uk

First published in the UK in 200⬛ ⬛⬛⬛ Books Ltd
PO Box 520, Weston-super-Mare, ⬛ ⬛⬛⬛, UK
email: submissions@oktoberbooks.co.uk
www.oktoberbooks.co.uk

A catalogue record of this book is available at the British Library.

ISBN-13 978-0955772832

Printed by the MPG Books Group in the UK

Television Killed Advertising

Paul Ashby

Edited by Edward Keating

www.oktoberbooks.co.uk

Firstly my special thanks to my wonderful wife, Remedios (Remy). Without her sensitive encouragement to persevere, this book would never have seen the light of day. I also must not forget a debt of gratitude to Alan Kirkland who had the patience and the wit to ensure that I completed this project on time. And a very special "thank you" to our daughter Anna (KK) Ashby for reading and re-reading this time and again for errors etc... my thanks to you all.

Contents

A new hope:
Foreword by the Editor

I was once told a cliché about advertising and marketing agencies. This was back when I was still a young journalist and the triple worlds of advertising, marketing and PR were a far-flung 'evil empire' which I thought I was valiantly (read: naively) crusading against.

The cliché went along the lines of: the agencies are full of bold young people under 40, bubbling and briming full of creative talent, inventing new and dynamic ways of communicating messages across to consumers. They are bright and talented, but almost all destined for burn out by the age of 40. New careers outside of the 'rat race' soon beckon in, what I am told are, more 'rewarding' fields.

But the cliché goes on to say every agency also has a white-haired legend who is a clear 20 years older than everyone else, has been there, done that, has a clear philosophy on 'communication' and cannot be phased by anything thrown at them by man, beast or client.

The white-haired legend is the font of wisdom, of inspiration and usually has a much younger partner and a sexy slick sports car. He or she is the Obi Wan to the Rebel Alliance of the agency.

Eventually, the naive young journalist succumbed and allowed himself to be 'seduced' by 'the dark side'. Once I crossed the floor, I discovered the three dark worlds of PR, advertising and marketing were part of the same yin yang as reporting, with no clear way of telling which was on the good side of the force or otherwise.

What I also discovered on the other side was the cliché is true. I believe the great beat writer Jack Kerouac once said: "Clichés are truisms and truisms are true." Seems the old boy was right.

In each place I have worked since leaving journalism, there have been these white-haired elder statesmen holdng the place together and guiding the flock of dynamic youngsters.

Paul Ashby is one of these elder statesmen. Inside these pages is his philosophy on communication.

Edward Keating
Marketing Consultant
(Aged 32, not currently seeking 'rewarding' work outside communications...)

Author's preface

Advertising is still with us... just. This is not a whimsical statement rather, advertising is still with us because the practitioners of advertising cannot see the way forward. It is also still here because certain people, on a diminishing scale, still believe advertising, in the traditional sense, works.

Let me state my prejudice right here and now... it doesn't, at least not to the extent previously believed.

Advertising was part of a period of the most radical transformation the world has ever seen.

Most of us have heard the oft quoted statement, "50 percent of my advertising is wasted. The trouble is I don't know which 50 percent."

In the 1980s I got to know a guy who maintained, when we discussed that oft quoted mantra, that in his opinion, more like 85 percent of his advertising budget was wasted.

Today, I believe for some clients the wastage can be as high as 100 percent.

I believe I am from a generation which has seen the last of advertising, as we know it. From now on, it will be largely hidden from our view as technology, alongside a far greater understanding of the communication process, allows the consumer to 'talk' to manufacturers. In turn, the manufacturer will accede to the customer's request.

The turning of the new century has seen the gradual awakening, on the part of manufacturers, that there are far more effective means of reaching out to, and communicating with, their existing customers and potential new customers.

I am sure that everyone's perspective will be different on what I am about to say. The affect, and therefore the success of advertising, has been grossly exaggerated in the past.

Some people think this exaggeration has been propagated by the media itself in an attempt to keep the good times, in terms of ad revenue, going.

A good example of this perpetuation is the claim which is resurrected with monotonous regularity in the business press, "British advertising is the best in the world." Every time I see this claim I cannot make any sense of it at all. How do they measure 'British' advertising against all else to arrive at such a ridiculous conclusion?

I have relied upon a good deal of research and the books of others as my bibliography shows and, at the same time relied upon my own experience as a major pioneer of interactive communication to the marketing community. I have therefore drawn upon more than £5 million of independent research available to me to substantiate my thesis. After all my technique of interactive communication is, to my mind, the most researched communication concept in the history of mass communication.

Before I go into detail on my techniques, let us look at the key premise on which I build my argument: Television Killed Advertising. Consider this, in 1987 the expenditure on advertising was $200 billion, more than the gross national products of Denmark, Finland, Ireland, Israel and Kenya added together, and the bulk of that expenditure was entirely wasted. Today, 2008, this advertising expenditure has risen to over $400 billion and is still rising, and still largely wasted.

Renaissance Communications
bringing communication back to marketing

Communication should be a two-way process. We can make sure you have proper dialogue with your customers. By building a proper relationship through real interaction you can increase sales.

We have a proven and completely accountable technique which will minimise the sales impact of media while allowing you to make spending cuts. Applying our methodology has been the foundation of the tremendous sales growth we have achieved for a range of blue chip companies.

Contact us at:

info@tvtag.co.uk

www.tvtag.co.uk
www.renaissancemarketing.co.uk

Television Killed Advertising

Communication and witchdoctors

I agonised about the decision to commence this book with a true story about witch-doctors, African and Western.

Then the penny fell, what better way to illustrate the point I hope to make. The fact that the business world has been misled by a gang of witchdoctors for a long time now, a gang that used modern totems to mislead and misinform business-men and women throughout the world.

In the not-too-distant future people will be absolutely appalled and, at the same time, amused, that we actually believed advertising worked to the extent we were told. No government in the world has been elected as a result of an advertis-ing campaign, despite all the honours bestowed and the huge financial success of a very well-known English advertising agency. However, we will discuss that monu-mental PR coup later.

Anyway, on with my true story....

I had been in Johannesburg for two weeks, having joined one of the coun-try's leading advertising agencies, VZ Advertising. I was still extremely new to the country and its strange ways, especially in the field of politics.

Amongst the clients I was working with were the prestigious South African Breweries. I was working on the accounts for Lion Lager, Lion Ale and Lion Export Ale, a premium beer.

We and SA Breweries' other advertising agencies had been informed by the then Chairman of SA Breweries, that we were to attend a meeting at their head-quarters in Commissioner Street on the Friday to meet with Doctor Ernst Dicter, the father of motivational research. Our modern day Western Witchdoctor.

There, we would have the fortunate experience of having Dr Dicter criticise our respective advertising campaigns. At this time, SA Breweries employed three advertising agencies. All their respective senior executives would be attending this same meeting.

My boss, Max Schultze, was fairly critical of the decision to hire Dr Dicter. Afterall, he was charging any client, and there were quite a few, $6,000 for an af-ternoon critiquing other people's work. Here was a transplanted European living in America, coming to Africa to tell the local advertisers how to communicate with the local population.

Max summed it up the best he could: "Another $6,000 out of the media schedule." Please bear in mind, $6,000 was a substantial sum of money in those days.

So, we dutifully went to the meeting, held in the sumptuous boardroom of SA Breweries. Full of a veritable who's who of South African advertising and market-ing. The Chairmen of Grant Advertising and PN Barrett with their assorted hench-men, together with all the marketing staff at SA Breweries. All in all, a total of around 25 people. And, at the head of the boardroom table, like a veritable God, sat Dr Ernst Dicter.

And, from two until 4.30 in the Johannesbugh afternoon, the honourable Doctor tore our advertising efforts to shreds, especially our campaigns for the African market.

All in all, a very profitable and easy way to earn $6,000. At the end, the Chairman of SA Breweries stood up and said: "I am sure that we would like to thank Dr Dicter for a most constructive and informative afternoon. We plan to reconvene this meeting a week hence, by which time you will have had time to consider what you have heard and then you can ask Dr Dicter questions. Additionally, Dr Dicter will tell us what he thinks are the important issues creatively we have to address when we advertise to the African market."

"Another $6,000 from the media schedule," muttered Max as we rose to leave.

A week later, I entered the offices of VZ at the bottom end of Twist Street at 8.30 in the morning. Max was in his usual position, reading the *Rand Daily Mail* in the foyer of the agency.

"Ashby", he said.

I went over to him. "Yes, Mr Schultz?"

"I want you to take my car and Edward," his Zulu chauffeur, "and go into Soweto Townships and get me a witchdoctor, in full regalia. He must have his bones. Have him appear at SA Breweries boardroom at precisely two o'clock this afternoon."

I guess when reading this today it sounds fairly simple and straightforward. Not so then. Firstly, it was illegal for a white person to enter Soweto without a permit, and they were not easy to obtain. Secondly, there was a certain amount of danger for an unaccompanied white person in Soweto.

Please remember, it was now only my third week in the Republic. However, mine not to reason why, mine but to do or die.

I went downstairs and spoke to Edward, who was a charming young Zulu, who just happened to love the Modern Jazz Quartet, a good starting point for both of us.

We set off for the townships and, along the way, I told Edward my instructions. He was amused and concerned at the same time. Witchdoctors had, and still have, great power within most societies, whatever name they go under.

To cut a long morning short, I had a fascinating time, I visited witchdoctors training schools as well as herbalists, and eventually we discovered a witchdoctor who was prepared to come with us, in full regalia and with the bones, for a relatively small fee.

He entered the Rolls Bentley and off we set. I must admit, as we neared the white business section of Johannesburg, I became more and more mortified. To start with, our guest, in full regalia, was starting to look a little out of place. And then I thought perhaps Max didn't mean me to be successful in my attempt and had merely engineered this so he might have a good story to tell.

We entered Commissioner Street in downtown Johannesburg, as we approached the imposing entrance of SA Breweries I was feeling distinctly uneasy.

Upon entering the building, all the African staff immediately disappeared. After all witchdoctors are immensely powerful and nobody wants to get on the wrong side of one.

We entered the elevator and rose to the 20th floor. Upon leaving the elevator, we went to the entrance of the boardroom, by which time I was feeling distinctly queasy. I softly knocked on the door, hoping against hope that nobody would hear me and I could disappear and claim that I tried but couldn't enter. No such luck. "Come in," said a voice, I half entered. Again there was a veritable who's who of the South African marketing community all looking at me, I caught Max's eye, "Have you brought him?" he mouthed at me. I nodded, he rose and approached the door. "Come in" he said to my witchdoctor. To the amazement of the people present, in came our witchdoctor, in full regalia, clutching his bones. Max took him by the arm and led him to the head of the table where Dr Dicter sat. Then Max said: "Doctor Ernst Dicter, the witchdoctor of Madison Avenue, I would like you to meet the witchdoctor of Soweto Townships."

To cut a long story short, Dr Dicter was never used again by SA Breweries and Max eventually landed the Castle Lager business, the largest billing brand within SA Breweries.

This book is dedicated to the witchdoctors of the advertising industry. I am full of admiration for the way they have operated, yet I am critical of the way they have wasted billions of pounds and dollars and other currencies, all the while not addressing the true meaning of communication. If they had, I truly believe the commercial world would be a better place than it is right now.

Riots are best?

Maybe riots are a better form of communication than advertising? So, where are we going with this chapter I hear you ask? Well it's back to Johannesburg and, yet again, Max Schultze, for this amusing story... please stick with it, there is a purpose in the telling.

The Johannesburg City Council had, in it's infinite wisdom, elected to ban Lion Export Ale for sale in the (black) townships. The reason? Simply, it was a premium beer sold in a 10oz bottle rather than the standard 12oz bottle. The council, with the wisdom only councils seem to possess, did not want the Africans paying a premium price for less beer. Despite the fact they would be receiving more of the active ingredient (alcohol) for their money.

South African Breweries called their agency VZ, where Max Schultze was CEO, and asked for advice as to how to handle the situation.

It should be noted here, in those days, unlike today with the TV obsessed advertising agencies, and to some degree, clients, agencies were called about anything to do with the communication of a corporation. This was because they supposedly understood what communication was all about.

The PR division of the agency was called in to discuss the best way to approach the issue.

Before anything was put into operation, Max called me into his office. "Ashby" he said, "I want you to go up to the creative department and have them prepare lots of banners, saying, in effect, 'Bring back Lion Export Ale'; and 'Banning Export Ale is racial discrimination'. Then go to Edward (Max's Zulu chauffeur) and have him hire several hundred Africans.

"Then I want you to issue them all with the banners and ask them to go into the townships and select their favourite bottle store (off licence) and parade up and down outside them. Mind you, I want no violence."

The next day the major (white) newspapers carried stories of peaceful demonstrations outside of the township off licences with photographs of the Africans (with their agency-prepared banners). It looked, and was, very effective.

Within a week, the Johannesburg City Council had rescinded the decision to ban Lion Export Ale and, within 10 days, township liquor stores were all carrying Lion Export Ale.

Much more effective than any form of one way advertising, or direct marketing programme, all that was required was an understanding of human behaviour, perception and interaction.

The point being, (or one of them, there are so many points that can be made with this story) Max was not an advertising man and he didn't certainly entertain the thought of needlessly spending his client's money in the vain hope of curing the problem through advertising. He applied an understanding of the communication process and human nature and solved the problem without costing the client thousands in ineffective advertising.

Campaign issued a supplement the other day on "media-neutral planning". I read the whole issue. Cover to cover, in the usual hope of finding something mentioned about the communication process. Many of the 'practitioners' had things like this to say: "Ideas are at the heart of this debate because they create genuine value for businesses. Agencies must become idea-centric." Or, try this for size: "The most profound insights, in terms of media-neutral planning, come from a blending of data and ad planning." Wow. Stunning stuff don't you think?

But, not surprisingly, none of the 'experts' had anything to say about the communication process or, for that matter, accountability.

So perhaps, we, the tiny band of individuals pursuing the true meaning of communications, should hold our own riots. We should have banners saying "Unfair to consumers", "What a waste of money". Or, how about, "Advertising is nothing more than a brand tax", "Television is the biggest waste of money for Brands", "Consumers don't read advertisements" and parade outside the large ad agencies and their clients' offices. Then maybe the appalling waste of time, undoubted but misdirected talent and money would gradually come to a halt. However, the words of Einstein come to mind: "You cannot expect the consciousness that created the problem to solve the problem."

When I told this tale and mentioned Einstein to an ex-agency man, now with a big multi-national client, he gave me the benefit of his wisdom, "That's assuming there is a problem."

Therein lies the real problem. Many people in advertising and marketing don't want to rock the boat. They certainly don't see what they are doing as a waste of time and an expensive drain on their client companies' profits. Somebody said to me not so long ago: "That is understandable". From their point of view, I guess so.

But, nevermind the existing people within the industry. For all our sakes we have to move on. Move on to a more pleasant, mutually beneficial, commercial world. Not ruled top-down but operated bottom-up for the convenience of all concerned, a truly interactive commercial society.

Advertising people, marketing people, clients, agencies all have to wake up to the fact the interrelated agendas of their huge powers have become utterly removed from the consumers they were originally created to serve. Their interests are now totally remote from our daily lives.

What is really odd, and frightening in a way, is the trade press, and the people they interview and mention in articles, all still cling to the past. To business stereotypes which are largely empty.

And the really weird thing, all these people mentioned in the trade press as today's experts on how to sell their client's products, still caricature their behaviour. Especially with the use of the word "creativity". Probably the most poisonous word in use today, certainly in the world of advertising and marketing. It has led us up a one-way street, wasting vast sums of money all in a desperate search for 'creativity'. Which, incidentally, has absolutely nothing to do with communication.

Television killed advertising

Ask any advertising person you know if they have heard of, or read, *The Cluetrain Manifesto* and most of them will shake their heads with an emphatic no. Which is a shame, because within this book lies the clue to their demise.

While the book is written with the web in mind, most of what it has to say is true of the communication process itself, whatever medium.

So, allow us to revisit *The Cluetrain Manifesto* and apply what it has to say about the world we live in now and the advertising and marketing world as we know it, setting aside the web for the moment.

In the 20th century, the rise of mass communication, the media, enhanced industry's ability to address even larger markets with no loss of shoe leather. Mass marketing truly came into its own.

With larger markets came higher rewards and these higher rewards had to be protected. More bureaucracy, more hierarchy and more command and control meant the customer who looked you in the eye, was promptly escorted out of the building by security.

The product of mass marketing was the message, delivered in as many forms as there were media and in as many guises as there were marketers to invent them.

Delivered locally, shipped globally, repeated inescapably, the business of marketing devoted itself to delivering the message. Unfortunately, what all these gurus of marketing did not realise, and still do not today, is that the customer never fully took delivery.

Why? Because there is no demand for these advertising messages. Let's face it, consumers don't want to hear from business.

The message that gets broadcast to you, me and the rest of the population has nothing to do with me in particular. Consequently, it's worse than noise. It's an interruption in my life and, like most people, I would rather do without it, thank you very much.

Just leave me to watch/listen to my programme without any interruptions. This is the awful truth about marketing and advertising. It broadcasts messages to people who simply don't want to listen to or see them.

Every advertisement, press release, publicity stunt and give-away designed by the marketing department, or advertising agency, is coloured by the fact all their hard work and planning is being presented to a public which doesn't ask to hear or see it.

In October 2002 the *Sunday Times*, in the UK, had this to say about the state of advertising, quoting Mike Moran, Commercial Director of Toyota (GB): "Things have changed a lot since you used to get 20 million people gathered around television sets to watch Coronation Street and one advertisement could reach them all.

"Marketing budgets are being spent differently, and this means less money is being allotted for advertising. A couple of million pounds can buy you a few hours on television but marketers are realising that it can buy an awful lot more if it is spent elsewhere."

Moran warns advertising agencies may be flatfooted in responding to the change: "Advertisers cannot find what they need from the big agencies, which tend to be biased towards television advertising. Small agencies are more flexible and open-minded to these changes, but the likes of WPP can be a bit slow to respond."

In 2002 Nestle, once one of the UK's biggest advertisers, slashed the amount it spent on television advertising. Andrew Harrison, its then Marketing Director, says: "This is a start of a trend towards more rounded communications. And the big agencies, like WPP, need to look at offering more than just the traditional services."

Despite all this rhetoric, there is no evidence yet of advertising agencies, or the marketing departments of clients understand the meaning of the word 'communications'.

And herein lies the real problem, the complete lack of understanding of what the communication process is all about.

Sending a message by itself isn't sufficient to create an act of communication, there needs to be a response to a message as well.

To illustrate this point, think of a radio station broadcasting late at night without a single listener tuned in. You don't have to argue about trees falling in an empty forest to agree that no communication has occurred here.

In the same way, when you have a speaker talking to one or more people who aren't listening, there is no communication taking place.

For communication to take place, you must have a message sender and a message receiver and the two sides must talk to each other to understand what the other is thinking/doing.

Advertising occurs when a group becomes too large for all members to contribute. One aspect of advertising is an unequal amount of "speaking". Advertisers deliver their information to the mass audience, with limited opportunities, if any, for feedback. The audience, therefore, is unable to talk back in a two-way conversation the way they might in a small group setting. As a result, they do not feel involved, do not feel the message has relevance to them as an individual.

Advertising views communication as something one person "does" to others. In this linear model, communication is like giving an injection. A sender encodes ideas and feeling into some sort of message and then injects them by means of a channel (television, newspapers, radio, etc.).

Despite its simplicity, this linear view of communication isn't completely accurate.

For one thing, it makes the questionable assumption that all communication involves encoding. A more obvious problem of the linear model is its suggestion that communication flows in one direction, from sender to receiver.

However, most types of communication, especially the interpersonal variety, are two-way exchanges.To put it differently, advertising's linear view ignores the fact receivers react to messages by sending messages of their own. And, if the original message sender is not listening in turn, what occurs?

Lack of communication competence.

Most advertising agencies and clients lack the skills of communication. Advertising messages are more carefully prepared than interpersonal communication and yet "message understandability" tends to be lower.

Advertisements are more carefully prepared because gatekeepers (those who prepare and send out messages) are more cautious about what they say to large audiences than they are to audiences of one or just a few people. They check their facts more carefully and they prepare their syntax and vocabulary more precisely.

And yet, because their audience contributes much less feedback, the source cannot correct any lapse in interest or understanding, so people are more likely to misinterpret what they hear or read through the mass media.

It is important to note, of course, that just because mediated messages are more carefully prepared, they are not necessarily more accurate. Gatekeepers have a way of looking at the world based on personal beliefs or motivations. This 'world view' sometimes tends to make media messages inaccurate.

Advertising ignores communication theory.

As the mass media has matured, the behavioural dynamics of perception and interaction, which are not addressed by advertising agencies, have become critical to the re-definition of media and its role in marketing communication. With passive one way forms of advertising, such as media display or television advertising, there is a certainty of a degree of non-responsiveness.

However, with interactive marketing communication techniques, there is a commitment to participate, which, in turn, leads to a set of possibilities, which are significantly different in how they affect the communication process itself.

All advertising is a form of learning, with the advertiser asking potential customers to change their behaviour once they have understood the benefits of the product or service on offer.

The anticipation of response generated through interactive marketing communication, means the recipients will approach the data with a commitment to read and learn it.

In other words, interactive marketing communication turns passive advertising into active advertising and actually alters behaviour during the learning process. It also cuts through the psychological barriers, which prevent an individual from changing brands.

People tend to filter out information they do not want to hear and this alters the effectiveness of advertising in quite a dramatic way. The purchaser's decision is invariably a compromise and this leads to a certain amount of anxiety.

The worry is that perhaps the purchase decision was not the best or right one. In order to minimise this anxiety, the purchaser seeks to reinforce their choice and begins to take more notice of their chosen product's advertising.

And, at the same time, the purchaser deliberately suppresses data, which might challenge their personal decision, by ignoring the advertising of competitive brands.

People are often loyal to a brand simply because they do not want to readdress a decision that they have already made. The opportunity to screen out such undesired data always exists when media advertisements have to stand on their own and fight for attention.

Despite all this, let's repeat what we suggested at the beginning of this chapter, there is still no evidence yet that advertising agencies, or the marketing departments of clients really understand the meaning of the word 'communication'. They are making progress in some areas, but there is clearly a whole lot more to be done.

So why call my book *Television Killed Advertising*?

Before, commercial television advertising agencies were responsible for producing everything associated with marketing a client's product, from aids for the sales force to packaging design and point of sales, plus many other tasks, thus cementing thier long-term relationship with clients. Along came television amd happily, very happily, advertising agencies, mistakenly, gave all of this up to pursue the holy grail of commercial television. Only they were mistaken, it was a poisoned chalice rather than the holy grail.

In the next chapter, I cover in detail the wonton destruction of agency's core business thus, *Television Killed Advertising*.

Employing an ex-ad agency person

Boy have they got problems. There are more of them around these days looking for work, preferably with a client, which begs the question, why?

Winston Fletcher, one of the grand old men of British advertising, had this to say recently in his book, *How to Capture the Advertising High Ground*:

"Agency giants are being cut to size by specialist rivals. The largest advertising agency in Britain employs just 310 people. Not long ago the largest agencies employed 1,000 or more. Advertising agencies are shadows of their former selves."

This has nothing to do with any short-term advertising recession. It reflects a long-term downward slide. In total, advertising agencies employ about half as many people as they did in the 1960s. In recent years, as advertising has boomed, advertising agencies have dwindled.

What is the explanation? Quite simply, advertising agencies do a lot less than they used to. They do almost nothing but create television commercials, press adverts and billboards.

While they continue to boast about their billings, the huge sums spent on the space and time to display their creations, they are no longer responsible for this expenditure.

It has largely become the preserve of media buying specialists. In 1975 media specialists bought one percent of all advertising. Today they buy 85 percent. This seismic change has slashed agencies' turnover.

Buying media is just one of many things agencies no longer do. Although many outsiders do not realise it, modern advertising agencies do hardly any package or logo design, direct mail, basic market research or public relations. They produce no in-store display material, design no brochures, build no exhibition stands, devise no sales promotions, and shoot no corporate videos.

Agencies have ceded strategic planning to management consultants. New product development and brand positioning are done by product and brand consultancies. Agencies failed to seize the opportunities offered by digital and interactive media, which have been cornered by young specialist companies. All this has fermented much discontent among the agencies' largest clients.

At the Incorporated Society of British Advertisers' Conference in 2001, there was disagreement between Carol Fisher, then CEO of the Central Office of Information, and Bruce Haines, President of the agency trade association, the Institute of Practitioners in Advertising.

Speaking from the platform, Haines lamented the decline in fees paid by clients.

Fisher, responsible, at the time, for the largest advertising budget in Britain, responded that as long as agencies continued to do nothing but create adverts, while ignoring the cornucopia of alternative marketing communication available, they did not deserve another penny. The shrinkage in advertising agency services, and the consequent reduction in their size and power, has partly been their own fault, but it has also been exacerbated by clients who have constantly whittled away at their remuneration.

As a result, agencies have shed virtually all of their ancillary marketing services (which their clients do not see as ancillary at all) for two cogent reasons: they are unable to do them well and they are unable to make money from them.

They cannot do them well because the best specialists no longer want to work for them. Advertising agencies are obsessively focused on creative people and their adverts. The creatives strut their stuff and everyone else is there to buttress them.

Naturally, people who are good at other aspects of marketing do not enjoy skulking in the admen's creative shadows. In agencies they feel like second-class citizens, leading them to leave and set up their own shops.

Clients have aggravated the situation by slashing the agencies' income. In the 1980s, most agencies received 15 percent commission on their clients' advertising outlay.

Now they are lucky to receive eight percent to nine percent from big spenders and less from many others. The 15 percent commission, which was universal, forced agencies to compete with each other by offering clients a package of marketing services, such as sales promotion, package design and new product development, either free or for a minimal fee.

The management of agencies offered these loss leaders because they could afford to and it was well worthwhile for all parties involved. They invented a name for themselves to explain the multiplicity of benefits they provided: the full-service agency, it could have been a new Oliver Stone movie.

Nowadays, nobody talks about full-service agencies. There aren't any. The provision of diverse marketing services has moved from advertising agencies to marketing conglomerates - holding companies such as WPP, Omnicom and Interpublic.

These conglomerates own a plethora of specialist companies, which handle all aspects of marketing. Outsiders think the conglomerates are just grandiose advertising agencies, but they are not. The most successful adman in Britain, WPP Chairman Sir Martin Sorrell, is not an adman at all. Never has been. Today, nobody has heard of the bosses of most advertising agencies. They are small, craft companies mostly owned by the conglomerates.

Curiously, neither the agencies nor their clients seem to have cottoned on to this new reality. Both sides look back wistfully to the glory days, when advertising agencies were 'full-service' (and wallowed in the commissions they were paid).

Today, many clients, like Carol Fisher, want them to co-ordinate the multiplicity of communication media available. There is no reason why advertising agencies should do this.

They are not paid to do it, the other specialists do not want them to do it and, despite their protestations to the contrary, I do not believe they do not know how to do it. British agencies are world leaders in advertising creativity (whatever this misbegotten statement means). They do what they do immensely well but what they do is immensely specialised. The marketing communication clock is not broken but it cannot be turned back.

Mass markets were fragmenting for many decades before the internet came on-stream and, since then, the net has enormously accelerated the fragmentation. No more can broadcast advertising shape the tastes and desires of an undifferentiated mass market.

Ideas create new markets. Unlike market research, true interactive communication in many forms provides a more immediate way to find out if those product ideas are any good.

Mass media was created to serve the marketing requirements of corporations.

Today, corporations must establish more intimate relationships with markets because that is where the knowledge is. Engaging in 'conversations' with relevant markets will become an important source of knowledge and innovation.

The quality of this market intelligence has already proven to be more accurate than conventional research and will help determine market share. This will accelerate in the future.

Without interactive communication, efforts to create new products and markets will continue to take place in a vacuum.

As manufacturers' products come to reflect the information provided through the genuine conversations of interactive communication, instead of the ballyhoo and adversarial marketing tactics that poses as marketing today, companies will be far better served and so will their customers.

Oddly enough, with interactive communication, companies can have everything they've always wanted. Greater market share, customer loyalty and so on. All the empty promises that advertising has been promising its clients but failed to deliver.

This big business, with its handmaidens, advertising and marketing, have created mass media.

And the biggest mass medium is broadcast, for which, read Television. And that is command and control management, complementing big business thoroughly. Both are all about imposing control top-down and both are driven by ratings, research and cost-per-thousand.

Sadly for big business and the broadcast media, people are turning away from broadcasting in their millions. Why? For a number of reasons.

They have acquired other interests and concerns, which broadcast is not providing for. And, most importantly, people are heartily sick of the sterile pronouncements of corporations and broadcast media. And especially of advertisements. No longer are they affected by the old slogan that used to appear in shopping outlets, "as seen on television". Those days are over, if indeed they ever existed.

Current methods and practices in marketing are still based upon a long past society of mass communication with no regard for individual customer needs and, as such, are in terminal decline. The fact is, markets are changing a lot faster than marketing, with the result that most marketing plans are obsolete before they have been written.

What most marketing departments fail to realise is we continue to move into a new marketing age. This new age respects the fact people in general don't trust business, they find it insulting and demeaning to be so cynically manipulated and they are feeling this way in greater and greater numbers.

There is an old adage in technology: "Intelligence always moves to the edge of the network."

The same is true of most other things, especially advertising and marketing; there are far more intelligent ideas outside of advertising agencies and marketing departments.

Existing advertising agencies are happy with current monopolistic profits and their general situation, so they badmouth any new idea, which threatens their incumbency or profits, or both. Advertising agencies are usually in denial until their profits are really threatened.

Just how dumb are they? The entire history of commercial television appears to have been a big plot erected on control from above rather than choice from below. Consumers have then been coerced into watching programmes in which they have no real interest. The advertisers who pay for the commercial break believe, on amazingly weak evidence, that some great percentage of people actually watch their commercials.

The television advertising business is a science based on suspect data. Traditionally, this data is based upon a small sample, which decides how many households watch an actual programme, and doesn't even measure the commercial break. Some advanced digital systems can track how many homes are tuned into a certain channel at any one time. However, the fact the set is on does not and cannot guarantee the programme and, more importantly for the advertiser, the commercial break is being watched. And it cannot tell you how many people are watching each particular television.

The way forward is through implementing interactive marketing communication programmes; all the problems of the past will disappear when this occurs.

The business formally known as advertising

With the huge changes about to occur, corporations are going to have to do a complete about-face.

A very large proportion of media functions will no longer be delivered top-down, as in the broadcast model. Instead they will be coming bottom-up, from the very customers most corporations are trying to 'order' to buy their product right now.

Business created mass markets through broadcast advertising, the same bossy voice of command-and-control it used on workers, however, in this instance, applied in the market place. "Just do what you're told" is not that much different to: "buy our products".

And you could effectively tell people to keep quiet, because that element of a conversation was banned in broadcast media, there was never a way to ask questions. A 30-second television commercial was never an invitation to converse.

In 1997, the respected advertising and media commentator, John Billett, had this to say in *The Times* newspaper in the UK, in an article titled, "Changing world puts focus on in-store action":

"The old view that advertising boosts a brand and trade promotions hurt it, is under fire.

"A combination of accelerating media fragmentation and dominant retailer concentration is turning conventional notions about the purpose of brand advertising and in-store trade promotions upside down. This raises questions about their respective contribution to the health of brands and profits.

"Conventional wisdom has it that trade promotions add short-term sales to a brand through increased trial and higher purchase intensity but lead to damage in the longer term through a cheapening of the price points and hence downgrade the brand image and lead to reduced profits.

"That same line of traditional argument cites media advertising as a life giving, sustaining brand force long term, maintaining and building sales for greater overall profit."

These oft-repeated mantras are based more on general belief and limited investigations. But they are increasingly being thrown into question by the wealth of rigorous analysis now possible via supermarket trading data.

A flawed promotion with the wrong pricing can lead to volume chasing for reduced profitability. Similarly, the failure to develop positive brand attributes in advertising can damage the brand.

However, there is little hard evidence trade promotions damage brands. Most successful brands run many trade promotions. Across the hundreds of brands we have measured, trade promotions can deliver short-term profitability without undermining long-term success.

Brands are not being held to ransom by avaricious retailers. Indeed, brands that manage and measure together both promotions and advertising success, prove the vital added value of promotions.

Needs will vary from category to category but, for brands with strong demand elasticity, promotions can attract non-users to buy, stimulate existing users to buy more and remind lapsed users to retry. That increased use can act as a reminder of the brand's values and stimulate further purchases after the promotion. If, on the other hand, the promotion attracts just predominantly deal buyers, but does so profitably, the promotion is still an effective marketing tool.

Although there will always be room for the misguided brand manager committed to a Bogof (buy one, get one free) for a brand with inelastic demand, letting consumers bring forward at a discount a purchase that would have occurred subsequently at a higher price, our tracking reveals that buying ahead is only a small metric in most promotion realities.

Our tracking of advertising effects, converting them into sales effects and measuring return on the investment shows advertising's worth is more subtle and sometimes invisible to the naked eye.

Advertising has a relatively weak sales influence, but its values can be far-reaching and are context-sensitive. As an investment, it has limited value short-term; its effects are only partially attributable and constitute a high risk. The problem for advertising is that cash financing is required quite independently of the incremental sales it generates. So, when company liquidity is attacked, we see cuts in media spend.

A trial in 2001 measured positive advertising effects delivering between £2.69 profit and £1.14 for every £1 spent, right through to a negative return of 28p for the £1 spent, a loss of 72p in the pound.

The tragedy for the media business is many brand managers and most advertising and media agencies are, in our experience, unprepared to calculate the contribution of advertising.

The range of promotional success and failure is also wide. We should expect trade promotions to be demonstrably contribution positive; the effects should be attributable and financed from margin in proportion to the sales generated, with limited demands on cash. Not all trade promotions meet these basic requirements.

We have examined the worth of trade promotion as a form of communication. Our conclusions so far are that trade promotions are communication neutral: the sampling effect of promotions cannot match per pound the reach of advertising; secondary location in store has no correlation with brand awareness (too much in-store clutter perhaps); and weight of promotional activity does not adversely affect quality perceptions. Promotions have to stand or fall by their profit and volume delivery.

Deal buyers exist and advertisers have to face the reality, they are a permanent feature in the marketing landscape. They are more aware and more informed than ever.

Advertising can also make for a high risk when compared with trade promotions. It is not surprising that the advertising budget is under more pressure in these times. This is not a threat to the overall role and value of advertising. It is a tough economic reality, however unpalatable to the advertising community.

Sir Martin Sorrell's plea in 2003 for marketers to reverse this trend, fails to appreciate the mounting evidence. Positive sales promotions meet customer needs and can add immediate contribution to profit in a way conventional advertising cannot, even if they are not cost-effective as a communication media.

Promotions and advertising have distinctive but complementary roles to play in well-managed brands. Extensive insight is required to determine the optimal balance of resources. Attempts by the advertising industry to raid a promotional budget do not, in my experience, influence commercially-minded managing directors battling to meet demanding targets. There is even a sense in which such arguments are counter-productive to the advertising industry, creating an enemy of promotions where there should be partnership.

Understand the word 'communication'

To start with, advertising people tend to think of it as 'message sending', and thus spend hours and hours crafting a message, primarily a 30-second television commercial and then arranging for it to be transmitted.

Marketing people are moving away from that totally inaccurate picture, however fast moving consumer goods (fmcg) marketing people still haven't cottoned on to the fact "you can sell more goods to less people, and still be more effective", that is if you understand the benefits of 'conversations'.

Media people, newspapers, magazines, television and radio lovingly call themselves 'the communicators" and say they "are in communications".

They are not. Never have been. All they do is prepare messages and then send them. They are most certainly not communicators.

They are totally unaware of those delightful words: cognitive dissonance; selective exposure; and selective perception. Wonderful words which, however, profoundly affect the meaning of our message and we ignore them at our peril!

However, it is the ego that chooses to ignore the word communication, the ego and that other overworked word 'creativity', hence the rush to hire, at greater and greater expense, the latest creative genius who is going to sell all those wonderful goodies. Utter rubbish.

Certainly, in this day and age of commercial clutter, creativity alone is no longer the answer, as if it had ever been, to the commercial needs of marketers. Creative genius is not the sole criterion for the success or otherwise of the marketing campaign.

So, let us examine the word 'communication' a little more closely.

In 2003, *The Times,* of London, defined communication as:

"Communication. n. 1. a transmitting 2. a) giving or exchange of information, etc. by talk, writing b) the information so given 3. a means of communicating 4. the science of transmitting information."

The interesting fact is the expression "the exchange of information". Communication is not a one-way flow of information. Talking at, or to someone, does not imply successful communication. This only occurs when the receiver actually receives the message which the sender intended to send. Message rejection, misinterpretation and misunderstanding are the opposites of effective communication. However, most advertising today depends on a single-step communication model:

A message sender → the message → receiver

This basic model assumes the sender is active, while the receiver is inactive or passive and the message is comprehended properly.

In this case, if the advertisement is creatively prepared and sent through the right medium and, if it cuts through all the other noise, and then if it is decoded correctly, the advertisement has done its job.

Declining faith in advertising

A new media age appears to be dawning, one in which many of the old rules of salesmanship will no longer apply.

It is hard to believe that anyone will sit still for numbing repetitions of intrusive jingles, or for 30-second spots of unrewarding commercials.

In the world of today, a world where people can talk back to their television sets, the age-old question of just how advertising works, and whether it works at all, may finally be answered.

Conventional mass media is a weak conductor of knowledge and comprehension. This is because it is a non-interactive communication vehicle. Communication research shows interaction raises the learning effectiveness of a piece of communication. Advertisers must search for and use an innovative mass media which provides interactive communication.

Otherwise, they have little chance to effectively generate in the target consumers quality awareness or communication learning.

Farewell to the passive television ad of old.

Viewers are becoming impatient with television's linear flow and are increasingly using the limited opportunities available to them to avoid the intentions of advertisers and programme makers.

Even though to many, the remote control is a fairly recent development, 44 percent habitually use it to dodge ads and 14 percent to watch two programmes at the same time.

Too much advertising is focused on a market place that is gone. Manufacturing has changed. Marketing has changed. Advertising has not, and it is no wonder clients seem to be losing faith in it.

This decline in confidence has been going on for several years, and the recession of 1992/93 brought it to crisis level. Advertising's share of promotional expenditure for packaged goods has gone from 43 percent to 25 percent since 1981.

This sense of declining effectiveness is due, in part, to an earlier perception which over-estimated advertising's power. In the industry's days of dominance, people believed it could change the ways consumers think and behave, not just influence them to favour one brand in a category they were already considering.

In earlier days, there was a faith that when there was little objective difference among products, an emotion-laden image was always used as a motivator.

Much of this sense of advertising's enormous power, and the almost inevitable effectiveness of image advertising, grew as mass advertising followed mass manufacturing in the 1950s and '60s. Mass manufacturing led to one-size-fits-all products. Local, individualised, and speciality products disappeared, and mass consumerism was achieved via mass advertising.

Now, customised products are coming back. Modern manufacturing has attained the ability to replicate, in its own way, the old world of choice.

Products are modified to meet many different consumer needs, including diet, health, ecology and economy among others. This technological revolution in manufacturing has made every vendor customise their product line.

Taking the place of undifferentiated brand products are various related lines of different choices for a consumer to select from. In this situation, our ability to sell everything under the umbrella of a single brand image has become limited and suspect.

How much can an ad lacking information really accomplish? Brand image is no longer the be-all and end-all of marketing.

With this vast differentiation, especially with high-ticket items and durable goods, buyers are looking for more than brand rhetoric. While consumers still buy chocolate bars or sports socks casually, as we should, without great forethought or analysis, consumers buy important expensive durables only after they have properly processed the information they need.

One of the major sources of this information is, or should be, advertising.

Here's the problem: Image advertising doesn't give us the information needed to buy knowledge-driven products. Since it doesn't help us, we have long since acquired the habit of tuning it out.

There is another aspect of advertising today which contributes to its crisis of confidence among marketers.

While marketing accepts significant effort must be paid to retaining a brand's current customers, too many advertisers consider such efforts boring and insufficiently creative, not something fundamental that needs to be done year in and year out.

The result of this thinking generates advertising which is all image and no content, designed for a mission that many regard as futile - the search to transform non-buyers into first-time buyers in the name of market expansion.

Marketers recognise how much has changed since the 1960s. For one thing, consumers do not pay attention to advertising the way they used to. The average British adult is already bombarded with 3,000 marketing messages a day. So it is nigh on impossible to get any one message noticed or remembered amid the entire clamour. One of our real concerns is we have an inability to stand out.

With good reason. Market research shows viewer retention of television commercials has slipped dramatically in the recent years. In 1986, 64 percent of those surveyed could name a television commercial they had seen in the previous four weeks. In 1995, just 48 percent could. And, in today's difficult and hostile market place the situation is much worse.

Even when consumers do notice an ad, they are less interested in the brand message it conveys. Consumers once clung to brands. They were Pepsodent households and Colgate households, families that washed with Persil and ones who bathed with Lux. And the characters Charlotte Street dreamed up to sell brands became pop-up icons.

Now, many British, who grew up on a steady diet of commercials, view advertising with cynicism or indifference. They are far more likely to buy on price rather than flash advertising messages. They are a lot less smitten by Kellogg's or Heinz.

There is little use for media planning that employs smaller and smaller units to use more and more media, all with the goal of bigger and bigger numbers. These are measurements which are rampant with abstractions and dubious assumptions. They are called such things as reach, gross rating points and unaided brand awareness. The result is to take media audiences which are flourishing with vitality and individuality and treat them as undifferentiated peas in a pod.

As a result, just as vendors have the greatest need to provide information and explain product attributes, the space and time units needed to do the job have become increasingly shorter and smaller. The only right answer is to change how we advertise. We need the constraint of picking fewer media and doing bigger jobs in them.

Advertising has been clinging to a world which existed 10 years ago as if it were trying not to notice it's vanished. Advertising has to modernise and change.

Its effectiveness will regenerate itself because the information content of advertising is a fundamental necessity for the efficient conduct of a complex and free market place.

Instead of asking: "When are the good times coming back?" we should be applying ourselves to doing advertising in ways which are right for the time we live in.

Now, let's look at the changing fortunes of media.

Newspapers and television have lost their exclusive hold on the advertiser. Where newspapers used to get advertising from every merchant in town, now they scarcely advertise at all. And the number of print and electronic advertising channels has substantially increased, such as pre-printed ad booklets stuffed in letterboxes or hung on doorknobs, local cable TV shoppers and direct mail.

In television, cable, satellite and other outlets have reduced the audience share of the networks and the outlook is for a further decline, say experts.

What has surprised everybody is the hyper-speed at which technology is moving. It is a monumental trend. More advanced forms, digital two-way systems, are now vying for approval.

The only question is: How do I structure my business so at least I'm a survivor, if not a beneficiary?

For newspapers, it means a combination of innovation and economy. Newspapers will have to target readers and bring advertisers, especially small retailers, more specific information on whom they are reaching.

Now broadcast television faces an avalanche of cable and other choices. The networks stopped financing technology decades ago, reasoning they had less need for technological capability because they were marketing companies.

Now technology threatens to steal their market, they have been kicked into action and innovations like the BBC iPlayer download are appearing.

Still, you may ask, who needs 150 or600 channels? Nobody is asking for them, but when they come they will be used. To begin with nobody asked for electricity or radio or television either, yet they have transformed every corner of the globe.

Marketing plans will soon be customised to every household. The technology is just about here. It is only a question of when people will accept it.

About 30 years ago, a national advertiser needed only to place a television spot on *Saturday Night at the London Palladium* and perhaps some ads in *TV Times* and *Woman* magazines to pretty much cover all the bases. But just as television and magazines have changed, so has the world of advertising.

Ads cost more than ever today, and they face a world of competitive clutter in which most get ignored. At the same time, with all the mega-mergers, leveraged buy-outs and bankruptcies among the big retailers, the number of major advertisers continues to dwindle.

To many marketers, the reason is as simple as it is scary - advertising has a permanently diminishing role in the selling of goods and services. Cynical consumers are wearying of the constant barrage of marketing messages. They are becoming less receptive to the blandishments of Charlotte Street and their loyalty to brands has eroded as they see more products as commodities distinguished only by price.

At the same time, consumers have changed, technology and the proliferation of media are transforming the science of marketing to them. Now, companies can increasingly aim their messages at carefully pinpointed consumers through direct mail.

Increasingly, when big companies see their business decline, they do not follow tradition and pour more money down the drain.

There is no denying that marketers want more accountability. Struggling to meet financial goals in markets which often grow no faster than the population as a whole, packaged goods companies have been leaning hard on their brand managers to produce quarterly sales results. The impact of image-building advertising on sales can often be tough to see. Not so with price discounts or coupons, which give sales quick, easily measured kick. People are saying: "I can't wait for advertising to work. I've got to turn these pounds around more quickly."

The ongoing challenge of the 21st century. How to reach your target market?

In many ways, television is an advertising, not communication, medium. As television declines in the face of competition from the new media, conventional advertising will decline with it.

'Advertising' is an outmoded concept, since media advertising is just one of many ways of communicating with customers, in an environment in which the balance of power is shifting in favour of the consumer rather than the advertiser.

Manufacturers and service providers need to look at ways of replacing the monologue of advertising with a dialogue which can also utilise a range of different 'relationship marketing' techniques: 0800 numbers, databases for micromarketing and so on.

The ability to boost sales automatically via advertising and promotion, taken for granted in the 1980s, has become a lost art in the 21st century. In an era of shifting consumer values and lifestyles, a cluttered communication environment and an overflow of information, niche marketing will become increasingly important.

Conventional mass marketing and advertising are based on the following assumptions:

- The right kind of awareness leads to positive attitudes;
- Attitudes lead to behaviour;
- People do what they say they do.

There is a problem, though - none of these are true.

As Don Shultz, the much quoted North Western University professor, observes: "There's no convincing evidence that attitude leads to behaviour, or that recall leads to purchase. There's lots of evidence that behaviour, in fact, precedes attitude, which knocks even more wind out of these tattered sails."

If these things are untrue, why do so many marketers believe them? Two reasons: The formula sounds logical and, until very recently, it just didn't matter what marketing assumptions you used. In the effervescent economy which gave birth to modern marketing, as long as you came up with a saleable product, let enough people know about it, and had an adequate distribution system, things worked out just fine.

That's hardly the case now. The difficulties of the 21st century have exposed the impoverishment of yesterday's beliefs - the sheer futility and astonishing waste of conventional methods are clear to anyone with eyes to see. The news is out and there's no going back. But this does not mean everyone is jumping on the bandwagon. Far from it, in fact.

Most of all, advertisers want information about the people most likely to purchase their products and they want to contact them directly. This is far afield from the expertise of most agencies. So, advertisers are increasingly turning to specialists in direct mail and telemarketing, and to database consulting companies.

The most important thing to find out is who your real prospects are. A great deal of advertising is wasted on people who won't buy the product. You cannot sell dishwasher detergent to people who do not own dishwashers.

To be sure of reaching the right audience, companies once had no choice but to use general advertising campaigns, which reach nearly everybody. Now, computerised market research is letting them collect detailed information on their customers, not just the approximation offered by demographics, but the specifics of name and address.

To communicate is to interact. As marketers, we are professional observers and communicators of our product message. All the technology we use is nothing more than a set of tools. All the messages we produce are simply by-products (written, recorded or filmed) of what we hope has been a successful effort in telling others, many others, what is important about our product.

Ironically, when we think about or describe two people talking with each other, the focus is on two persons interacting. The view is a behavioural one, focused on human activities, not on the medium of communication or on the literal messages produced. Perhaps this is because no machinery, no invented technology, is interposed between the two people involved in interpersonal communication.

However, when we shift from the simplest form of communication, two people engaged in a thoughtful conversation, to the more complex forms of mass communication, somehow our attention is distracted. We focus on the technologies interposed between the sender and the receiver and the sudden multiplication in the volume of messages dispatched.

These unfortunate distractions divert our attention from essential elements of the communication process. While technology and multiple messages are necessary elements in mass communication, they are far from sufficient for any actual communication to take place.

Communication results from an interaction in which two parties expect to give and take. Professional communicators, who ignore the characteristics and orientations of the audience members, do so at the peril of actual communication or information transmittal.

In other words, mass communication, if it is to be successful, must take on many characteristics of interpersonal communication. Audience members must be able to give feedback. Media practitioners must be sensitive to the information contained in the feedback. The give and take can result in understanding, or to put it another way, real communication.

Advertising agencies need to change their limited definition of communication and media and see themselves as specialists in a range of techniques.

The decline of the golden age of advertising agencies centred on the creative television commercial has commenced. Unless they wake up to the changes that are occurring, they risk becoming the first dinosaurs of the new media age.

What goes around, comes around

The 75th anniversary issue of *Marketing* was an interesting read.

I had eagerly grabbed a copy hoping it was going to reveal not only the past history of marketing and advertising in England but, and to me, more importantly, the exciting future which lay ahead.

Was I ever wrong.

There was not one mention of the word "communication", despite the fact, in my opinion, successful communication is what marketing is all about.

Rather, there was a self-congratulatory note, like the headline to one article "Changing Times, lasting truths."

Which said, basically: "The advertising industry has changed enormously in 45 years. Or has it?"

Then it went on to say: "...reading an article on choosing an agency in 1962 appearing in *Marketing* they found many of its recommendations relevant today." Really?

I don't think so at all. The communication scene has changed so much and advertising agencies are falling by the wayside. As the magazine says, consumer tastes, technology and media channels have all changed beyond recognition since the '30s, but the industry's core principles have remained remarkably constant.

Best summed up by the words "one trick ponies".

There was even an article on the success of BT, it contained this little gem: "Understanding and spelling out the importance of connections to our consumers has summed up BT's marketing efforts of the past 25 years, its strong history of popular advertising is testament to this." Really?

And there's the rub. Throughout this little 75th exercise there was not one mention of accountability. And one would have thought that, more than ever, at a time when the advertising aspect of marketing is under severe questioning as to its effectiveness, that a few, unquestionable research studies proving, once and for all, that advertising works, would be extremely well received.

But then again, and to the best of my knowledge, there is still not one research study that establishes conclusively that advertising sells products.

If you accept my thesis that the key to successful marketing is successful communication followed by successful selling, then allow me to insert here the correct definition of the word 'communication' and I would, at the same time, like to suggest that this should have been included in the 75th anniversary issue of *Marketing*.

What is communication?

After a little thought, most people come up with a definition that is about transmitting and receiving information. A little more thought might produce the word exchange. This is more satisfactory, but still assumes that communication is about moving something, about conveying, or sending, or delivering, some commodity called 'information'.

In fact, the word has quite a different root meaning. It derives from the Latin *communis*, meaning 'common'. Or 'shared'. It belongs to the family of words that includes communion, communism and community. Until you have shared information with another person, you haven't communicated it. And until they have understood it, the way you understand it, you haven't shared it with them.

Communication is the process of creating shared understanding.

Never once did this special edition of *Marketing* mention the fact that we must change in the way we think about media, there must be a major shift away from thinking about media as 'channels' down which we tip messages and information.

Neither did this issue of *Marketing* once seriously discuss research, especially focus groups, both of which consume vast amounts of marketing monies.

Never once did this issue consider the need for more patience. The more breakthrough, the more the revolutionary and the more innovative an idea is, the longer it will take for people to appreciate it.

Next, we feel that they should have pointed out that today, with all the clutter, mistrust etc., that exists, people in management need to tolerate uncertainty. The thing that's driving all this focus-group and market research data is the desire of people with the management power to make every decision as methodical, thought out and certain as possible.

Severe symptoms of what we call "Top-Down-Management."

These days and wherever you go, a revolution in media consumption is happening. Nobody in most traditional media businesses has a clue where it will end up, but the trick for existing brands will be to find ways to retain audiences and advertisers. In a era where people have the tools to rewrite and remix what they do not like, the unawareness of all this shone through the special issue of *Marketing*.

Certainly the next, and major, development within marketing is the development of interactive communication. Again, no mention of this most significant of all developments, so we think that this little description of interactive communication should have been included somewhere within this issue.

Defining interactive marketing.

Interaction can be defined simply as straight forward communication between two parties. Presently, we are in danger of losing the real meaning of interaction, as we tend to focus discussions on the emerging technologies and neglect the communication process itself. With an understanding of the real meaning of interactive communication, existing media can be made interactive, and subsequently far more cost effective

Branding is dead

If branding is the cause of advertising, what lies next for advertising? Because today, the deal trumps image every time.

After all, we're in the 21st century and venerable, once solid, brands are vanishing. And direct marketers are flourishing. If we look at the detritus of branding. Here's Levitt, a giant name in home building.[what?] Chapter 11, Levitt follows automobile brands Plymouth and Oldsmobile - Vanished. Then there's Intel, one of the most highly advertised brands with market share lost to chip producer AMD.

Then, there's Merrill Lynch. The giant revised its entire securities marketing structure to be able to compete with web upstarts. Now it is set to be swallowed by Bank of America.

And so it goes on. Compete or lose. Wal-Mart had a next to zero image and Sears had a next to 100 image. AT&T and Xerox had their universe to themselves. IBM owned the PC market. Kodak and Polaroid were riding brand-horses long after their steeds were dead. Jordache jeans were de rigueur. And so it goes.
The internet stamps across brand worship. The web is price-driven, and it has become the dominant sales medium, the new mantra is. Adapt or lose.

The "how much do you spend on advertising" advertising agencies interpret the whole concept of branding as brand awareness. However, today's potential customer, both in consumer and business, is very cynical. They are after a deal they can regard as reliable and certainly not a tribute to an arrogant, chest thumping, no-longer-competitive brand.

If branding spend were paramount, New Coke would have succeeded. It was an extension of what many regard as the best-known brand in the world. The Wednesday version of CBS-TV's "60 Minutes" wouldn't have flopped. Linux wouldn't have scored such a gouge into Microsoft's turf. Want me to buy your brand? What's your deal?

So, where next for advertising? Generating brand loyalty? Difficult? Ask any car dealer about how hard it is to hold on to the customers who used to trade in cars every three years but this year got an extra £100 discount from a dealer 30 miles away.

Total dependence on brand as a marketing force parallels a marketing student striving for an "A" when using lecture notes his grandfather scrawled during kinder, gentler pre-Future Shock times.

Outside it's freezing. You want ethylene glycol antifreeze in your car. Do you care which brand, as long as it's ethylene glycol?

You have a mild prostate problem. In the USA a prescription for Hytrin, on which Abbott Laboratories spent many millions of dollars, costs more than £100. A prescription for the generic, Terazosin, costs about £20. Your doctor and pharmacist probably suggest the generic. So do Wal-Mart and Target, which sells the generic for £4. Hey, but wait please, the generic has no brand, no image. Maybe not, but it has the primary contemporary incentive, price.

Perhaps combining brand with 21st century awareness is the Kingdom of Heaven, but that kingdom opens its borders to those who actually combine, instead of bowing to a personal prejudice based only on tradition.

In closing this section, may I say how surprised I am that direct and brand seem to be out of sync with each other. I find myself defending direct as a stand-alone, surviving when brand isn't a factor. Does direct need a defense? No. Does branding need a defense? Yes.

The attraction of interactive communication

Let's return to the prehistoric human fascination with telling tales. Since the beginnings of any civilised society, the marketplace was the hub of civilisation, a place to which traders returned from remote lands with exotic spices, silks, monkeys, parrots, jewels - and fabulous stories.

Interactive communication, properly executed, more resembles an ancient bazaar than fits the business models companies try and impose upon it.

People respond to interactive opportunities because they seem to offer some intangible quality long 'missing in action' from modern life. In sharp contrast to the alienation wrought by homogenised broadcast media, interactive opportunities provide a space in which the human voice could be rapidly rediscovered.

Unlike the lockstep conformity imposed by television, advertising, and corporate propaganda, interactive communication gives new legitimacy – and free rein – to play.

People long for more connection between what we do for a living and what we genuinely care about. We long for release from anonymity, to be seen as who we feel ourselves to be rather than the sum of abstract metrics and parameters.

We long to be part of a world that makes sense rather than accept the accidental alienation imposed by market forces too large to grasp or to even contemplate.

Remember the marketplace of old. Caravans arrived across burning deserts bringing dates and figs, snakes and parrots, monkeys, strange music and stranger tales.

The marketplace was the heart of the city, the kernel, the hub.

Like the past and the future it stood at the crossroads.

People worked early and went there for coffee and vegetables, eggs and wine, for pots and carpets. They went there to look and listen and to marvel, to buy and to be amused.

But mostly they went to meet each other, to talk and interact.

Markets are conversations.

So, what went so horribly wrong? From the perspective of corporations, many of which by the 20th century had become bigger and more powerful than ancient city-states, nothing went wrong.

Things did change however.

Commerce is a natural part of human life, but has become increasingly unnatural over the intervening centuries, gradually divorcing itself from the very people on whom it depends, whether workers or customers. The result has been to create a huge chasm between buyers and sellers.

Advertising's failure. Conventional advertising has failed the natural human need for social interaction.

We have created a media society during the past 30 or 40 years where there is an extraordinary reduction in interaction because of the one-way and more passive form of information that exists.

People desire to be taken account of, to affect change, learn and personalise their relationships with their environment.

These psychological and sociological factors are part of the incentive to interact with advertising. However, these tend to be minimised in the incentive direct response field, there are a phenomenal number of reasons which cause people to interact which go beyond just giving them things.

The one problem facing interactive advertising is the fact that it has become a cliché in recent years, without any clear or consistent definition of what the word means or how it is supposed to work.

Properly executed, it has none of the woolly theorising that lies behind the arguments about various forms of so-called interactive communication using direct marketing and electronic media (most of which involves at best the minimum of true interactivity).

The truth about your marketing gurus

Or, more importantly, how to increase your profits

There still exists today marketing people who maintain, to all and sundry, that they are really special, in fact they are the gurus of marketing.

We all know them, when I first entered advertising I used to think that these marketing people were really something else. They knew secrets that I would never be privy to. And yes, they looked extremely self-satisfied and smug and looked at you as if you were a complete and utter fool.

"Ah yes," they used to say, "But you're not in marketing, so you just don't understand."

Or, and this is worst of all and the ultimate sin, I think, in marketing communications: "I know that you cannot measure it. However, just trust me, I know it's working."

Thankfully for us all, but especially clients, those days are nearly over, nearly I said, there are still a few of them around.

The fact of the matter is, once you understand just how effective and accountable interactive communication is, then marketing, for whatever product or service, is not a secret, and allows your business to be carried out according to serious business principles.

The trouble is that your marketing people have become caught in the trappings of marketing, by that I mean the award presentations. Jetting off to attend a 'shoot' as if that is all that matters. In doing so they have completely forgotten their job is to sell a product.

This has resulted in many companies today regarding marketing as ineffective and, therefore, in many cases is considered to be strictly non-essential.

To prove this point, simply look at their actions. Whenever budgets are tight, marketing is one of the first budgets to be cut.

Once you come to understand the sheer effectiveness of interactive marketing communication, yes, you can cut your budgets by as much as half, and be far more cost effective and totally accountable. Now that is a piece of information most marketing directors and advertising agencies do not want to hear, for obvious reasons.

However, there are other problems that we have to attend to. Unfortunately many firms are rushing headlong into, what they regard, as interaction, without a clear understanding of what interactive communication is all about, or how to get their customer into a genuine long-term interactive relationship.

A major deficiency of many of these interactive approaches and programmes which have been implemented is, in actual fact, they have had very little to do with interactive communication and that such (failed) attempts have actually resulted in an alienation of customers.

We firmly believe that the discipline of interactive communication, properly executed, is a science and that spending on interactive marketing can be measured. And, more importantly, it needs to be, and can be, accounted for.

Interactive marketing also needs to be correctly understood.

If you think marketing is simply making great commercials and lifting sales by giving coupons, rebates and promotions, you're simply finished. You will never succeed. Ever.

At the moment marketing people, by and large, have forgotten that marketing is all about selling. It is not about creating an image. An image does not make people go out and buy your products. It most certainly is not about creating award-winning advertisements.

It is about results, and therefore, profits.

The only way we can go forward today is through interactive marketing communication. We must develop methods to create relationships between producers of goods and services and customers that have never existed in the past. According to Wilbur Schram, these relationships involve: "The mutual recognition of some special status between exchange partners."

Clearly, what passes for a relationship under the definition of many so-called interactive programmes is not likely to be an interactive programme in the eyes of your customer, in that it is mostly one-sided, lacking in true interaction, or two-way communication and most certainly lacking in any emotion.

It is becoming vitally important that a true standard be set for a genuine, understandable definition of interactive marketing communication.

Seven deadly sins of advertising

Facing the painful truth is the first essential step:

Sin Number one (And in many ways this is the biggest sin of them all.):

The total lack of genuine accountability and effectiveness. More and more evidence is emerging that there is ample justification for questioning a major advertising pretension that it does, indeed, work at all.

The repetitious cry and certain belief that "creativity" is the answer to all marketing problems – it isn't and frankly never really has been.

It's a given that all human knowledge is provisional but it is also incremental, the sum of what we know to day is far greater than 30 years ago – with, possibly, the sole exception of marketing/advertising. Nothing new has been added to the armoury of advertising. No debate is taking place as to where to go next. Perhaps that is because there is no place else to go.

However, today it is still an article of faith among advertising people that advertising will not change because, they say, it works.

Facing the painful truth is the first essential step in devising a sensible strategy for the perpetuation of advertising. And the painful truth is advertising no longer works.

Sin Number two:

There is too much advertising, which all seek to do the same thing in the exact same way. Our everyday lives are completely cluttered. How does one piece of marketing communication stand out from another?

Are advertisers not even considering this issue? Maybe for financial reasons, advertisers do not want to address the problem of clutter? It is a huge and growing issue which contributes to the declining effectiveness of all advertising.

The poor old customer, or in advertising speak, consumer, does not want to take delivery of even more messages. After all, they do not appear to be taking much notice of the messages that exist already.

The advertising world has de-humanised and de-personalised the process of communication and very little evidence of consideration of the consumer exists.

Sin Number three:

Advertisers just don't listen. Whenever some well-meaning person dares to question the 'advertising works' article of faith, down comes a torrent of unfounded responses and, the fact is, it can only be unfounded responses because advertisers do not have a solid fact to support their spurious claims. They should listen to their clients.

As one large advertising buyer (a client to the advertising agencies) explained to me: "In today's marketing landscape, building a brand is about a whole lot more than advertising. An advertising agency alone cannot deliver everything we need, even though agencies may claim to deliver this, its a myth."

Or, perhaps advertisers could even listen to people closer to home.

In a long letter in MediaWeek, following a conference in Wales, Derek Morris, Chairman and Chief Executive of ZenithOptimedia, said, among other things: "But what are the lessons to bring home from south Wales? What should we actually do? And there, in the final session, reality caught up when the client told us to 'change before you are dead'."

Sin Number.four:

If advertisers don't want to listen, then for Heaven's sake, they should at least try to forget the glorious past.

Their current model of advertising was developed in the 1960s when product choice was much more limited and people were easier to stereotype into categories like income, sex and class. It was much easier for advertisers to target people and bombard them with sales messages.

Today's marketplace is different and all the old certainties are gone. To be effective in communications, it is sound advice for advertisers to start with the premise they know nothing about the people they believe the product is aimed at.

Advertisers have all become too parochial, too introspective, too convinced by their own hyperbole.

Sin Number five:

Stop this insane rush onto what has been laughingly dubbed web 2.0. It is not a medium intended for mass advertising, and I agree with the premise that users became more or less desensitised to any advertising placed on Facebook and such like.

Clients are experiencing fast diminishing returns on their social networking ad investments. Clients are expressing disillusionment.

Web marketers, ranging from Google, at the apex of the ad triangle, to a mass of small companies, are showering social-networking sites with ad dollars. By all accounts these efforts are not bringing the hoped-for returns.

The question is not simply: 'Is the advertising model broken?' The question now is: 'What are we going to replace it with?'

The complacency of the IPA is overwhelming, it appears not to be doing anything to answer the increasingly strident complaints.

Complaints such as, clutter, and here the irony is that advertising agencies appear to think placing more advertisements is the way to solve clutter.

Complaints such as the lack of accountability, today, and after 50 years of extensive advertising, there are no reliable figures available on audience measurements.

And most certainly there are no effective studies as to the effectiveness of advertising on sales, as a return on investment (ROI) and much more.

Today it is more important that a close investigation as to the suitability of advertising on Web 2.0 be undertaken instead of rushing onto the net and ignoring all the signs. These are that it is a highly unsuitable medium for advertising.

After all it is 'The Wild West' where anything goes.

Sin Number six:

Advertisers inability to move rapidly into the post-advertising mindset is caused by them being unable to recognise Sins one through five above.

Astonishingly, a sizeable percentage of marketers and marketing-service leaders seem mired in the advertising mind-set.

In a transparent world, the power of an ad campaign to change minds is strictly limited, and getting more so every day. It's way past time for the industry's leaders to get naked and reinvent advertising. If they can.

Sin Number seven:

Advertisers have a complete and utter lack of understanding of the word 'communication' together with a lack of appreciation as to what can, and does, stifle effective communication.

All advertising is a form of learning whereby the advertiser is asking people to change their behaviour after learning the benefits of the products or services on offer. However, we all tend to filter out information which we do not want to hear. This clearly alters the effectiveness of conventional advertising in quite a dramatic way.

The final purchase decision is invariably a compromise and this leads to a certain amount of anxiety, the worry that perhaps the decision was not the best or the right one. In order to minimise this anxiety, the purchaser seeks to reinforce their choice and begins to take more notice of their chosen product's marketing communication.

Due to a lack of understanding of the communication process we have created a media society during the past 40 or 50 years where the whole process has been de-humanised.

There is now an extraordinary reduction in interaction because conventional advertising and marketing have become a one-way practice whereby information is disseminated in a passive form.

So what are the advertisers going to do about this?

An absolute disgrace

Why are they allowed to get away with no accountability at all?

The pollution of advertising messages is getting worse, despite supposed claims to clean the problem up.

Because advertising agencies have no answer to the problem of advertising's increasing ineffectiveness, the solution now is an increasing stampede to any new destination, like mobile phones where the greatest risk lies for a new avalanche of commercial content.

While all this is taking place, a big assault on television is underway by, for example, Google.

And all of this adds up to, you've got it, more and more clutter.

So while more and more marketing monies are poured down the black hole of television and internet advertising, there is another threat from the rackets and scams of the digital mafia.

The problem is so dire that hackers are now conducting online auctions for people's personal details. It has emerged there is an estimted $8 billion online black economy centred on credit card theft, corporate blackmail and insider share dealing.

Do you want your advertising to appear in such an environment? Meanwhile advertising agencies are leading the rush, together with increasing the clutter, onto that totally unproven, and highly suspect medium, the internet.

Even that well-known advertising personality, Jerry Della Femina, is on record as to questioning the value of advertising on the internet. Jerry has played an enormously influential role in the history of advertising. He states: "I don't know any advertising agency that has mastered the internet yet. Being able to understand it and sell products on it through advertising creates resentment, working to shut down attention rather than elicit interest."

For media companies, the problem of clutter raises complicated questions of economics. Media companies and their associates won't look at it because they don't think in a multimedia way. Advertising will have to try and deal with the problem.

And the new media has the potential to deliver even more saturation, clutter and intrusiveness than traditional media, so the new media will only worsen marketing resistance.

Any time there's a new destination for people, the assumption is they've got to find a way to put some ads there. That's only going to make things worse.

Under the headline: "The Money-waster That Marketing Ignores" *AdAge* had this to say about clutter's drain on advertising effectiveness:

"Clutter, the rising blizzard of commercial messages sweeping through TV shows and other traditional and non-traditional communications channels, has become a blinding, deafening force heavily cutting into the overall effectiveness of advertising."

AdAge paints a bleak picture of an industry apparently determined to ignore what may be its largest single money-waster.

However, the truth is that the interruption advertising model that supports television is broken, and without the utility that is currently found only on the internet, television will eventually become completely unsupportable.

People don't like to watch ads. The combination of the internet and PVRs have opened up a Pandora's Box. People know what life is like without the traditional advertising model, and there's no going back. They will willingly sacrifice some production quality if doing so means they don't have to be interrupted. Trying to force people to accept interruption is only going to turn them off more.

The death knell for the advertising agencies?

There is, and has been for some years, a very simple solution to the ills that beset the marketing and advertising industries. In the past, the advertising agencies have shunned the solution because it does not rely upon creativity, reach and frequency, the current model so beloved by the advertising industry.

It is interactive marketing communication. In one fell swoop, clients could solve all their problems and assist existing media in solve its at the same time.

Interactive advertising is richer than all other forms of marketing communication, and it is becoming increasingly clear that it is only a matter of time before clients embrace the business-saving life force of interaction.

Choose your own commercials anyone?

Interactive television will immediately halt the interruption model on which television is based: that is interactive marketing properly executed will make advertising on terrestrial television become richer because of the very nature of interactive marketing communication.

Existing terrestrial television needs no new technology imposed upon it to create immediately highly successful, totally accountable, advertising.

Oh no... not again

Periodically that old hoary story, 'subliminal advertising works,' appears in maga-zines and newspapers, probably as a space filler.

I do wish that somebody would put an end to one of the great advertising myths of the 20th century.

Media then chooses to editorialise about a non-running story.

The fact of the matter is that the whole story of subliminal advertising first broke in America. Two enterprising young men dreamt up the scheme, however the word "dreamt" is the key to the whole myth. That's all it was, a dream.

There was no research, there were no subliminal advertisements embed-ded in cinema movies, in fact the whole thing was a hilarious scam. That's all. But the damage it has caused is immense.

Firstly, let us review the role of advertising. Marketing applies advertising to the selling of goods or services, so, what is advertising? It is nothing more than a form of learning. The advertiser is saying to his audience: "Learn about my product/service and then please change or modify your behaviour."

Well then, what is learning?

Most educationalists today say that real learning is about answering a question or solving a problem. The questions can range from the immense to the trivial, however, when we have no questions we need no answers.

Apply questions and an understanding of human behaviour to the market-ing of products, then you start to have real communication taking place.

But, back to the damage it has caused.

Firstly, it makes it sound as if the process of advertising is far too easy. It is, to the extent that advertising agencies choose to ignore some human behavioural aspects of the communication process, those of selective perception and selective exposure.

Both of which invalidate most advertising messages.

How many times have I attended meetings where the Creative Director, in an attempt to justify weak creative thinking says proudly: "It is almost sublimi-nal..."

And the poor old client, judging that they (the advertising agency) are the experts, and they know what they are talking about, goes along with it. Committing millions again, into the non-accountable dustbin of advertising.

Of course, it contributed to the myth as to the invincibility of advertising, al-lowing advertising agencies to completely ignore the growing clamour for some form of accountability, which, in turn as brought us to the position we are in today.

Today's marketplace is different and all the old certainties are gone. To be effective in your communications, it is sound advice to start with the premise that you know nothing about the people that you believe your product is aimed at. Advertising has become too parochial, too introspective, too convinced by its own hyperbole.

However, when we shift our attention from the out-dated, discredited practice of advertising, and focus on its replacement, interactive communication, then all the old rules of the game, if there really were any, change.

Interactive communication, properly executed, more resembles an ancient bazaar than fits the business models companies try and impose upon it.

People respond to interactive opportunities because it seems to offer some intangible quality long 'missing in action' from modern life. In sharp contrast to the alienation wrought by homogenised broadcast media, interactive opportunities provide a space in which the human voice would be rapidly rediscovered.

But, from the client's point of view, Interactive Communication is far more cost effective, and allows clients the attractive opportunity to, substantially, reduce their horrendous advertising/marketing budget while, at the same time becoming far more effective in all of their communication objectives.

Which method do you choose?

Interactive communication or regular advertising?

The choice is yours.

"It's not sexy..."

Independent companies in Australia, the UK, USA, Japan, Singapore, New Zealand and The Philippines have extensively researched interactive communication the way I do it. A total investment of £5m has been made to make the technique totally accountable.

Numerous studies have been conducted to measure and document the sales impact of the technique. In point of fact, measurements are always made on the incremental sales generated by each interactive 'event' for every participating brand because the premise of my business is on making advertising expenditure accountable. The results are presented to each client as a post evaluation.

However, despite the fact advertising campaigns, by and large, are never accountable, I have had advertising agencies totally reject the accumulated £5million investment we have made in accountability.

One such example was at the presentation made to a well-known adevrtising agency, which was mentioned previously. Having completed a gruelling presentation to account directors and creatives as well as sales promotion people, one account director looked at me and said: "You might have £5million of research... but I have a feeling in my gut..."

I left that meeting knowing full well, in my gut, that I would never work with this agency. As a point of interest I have never, in 30 years, had one advertising agency as a client.

To demonstrate the effectiveness of the technique I use, below are some highlights of the technique and some research results from reports prepared by independent research companies in conjunction with past interactive programmes. But before the research results, I'll explain a little about interactive communication.

Interaction can be defined simply as straightforward communication between two people. Unfortunately, the real meaning of interaction is being lost as agencies focus their discussions on the emerging technologies and neglect the communication process itself. A truly interactive marketing approach to an advertising campaign can be achieved through game playing and programmed instruction. Considerable research has demonstrated this can result in greater consumer commitment to a product which, in turn, can create increased sales.

Interactive communication exists to communicate clearly an advertising message, using existing media, to an open, focused and receptive mind based upon the principle it is not what you say, but how your consumer interacts with what you say, which primarily determines how successfully the message gets across.

The changes in consumer perception and purchase behaviour produced by this form of communication are traditionally associated only with extensive advertising campaigns involving high levels of frequency and the inherent inefficiencies which result from such efforts.

Interactive communication consists of three important elements:

- Programmed instruction - dissects the logic of a communication into smaller parts. Asks the reader/viewer to think about and respond intelligently to each broken down statement, ensuring the consumer understands the 'whole' of the communication.
- Game playing - embodies the principle of game playing as learning to gain maximum consumer attention.
- Presented as an advertising 'event' - the advertising message is perceived as meaningful information rather than an interruption to the normal reading or viewing process.

Interactive communication alters the way people perceive advertising and will increase consumer awareness, increase message comprehension and increase sales.

Interactive Communication, properly executed, creates an open, focused and receptive mind, and will:
- Eliminate the problem of commercial clutter
- Increase advertising effectiveness
- Make all advertising more cost effective
- Make people receptive to the content.

So, here are some brief examples of the techniques accountability and effectiveness. There are hundreds of other uses for the process from politics to business-to-business. I detail only a few examples:

Client: Kellogg's
Brand: Rice Bubbles
Category: Breakfast Cereals
Country: UK
Year: 1987
Research by: AGB

"Among all main grocery buyers the following increases were achieved among those who saw the programme over those who did not. Prompted-Brand-Awareness + 8.8 percent; Past-4 week-purchase +41.7 percent and Next-Four-Weeks-Purchase +42.1 percent."
AGB.

Client: Kellogg's
Brand: Sultana Bran, Sustain, Special K, Just Right, All Bran.
Category: Breakfast Cereals
Country: Australia
Year: 1987
Research by: AGB

"All participating products showed positive growth (between 2.2 percent and 10.8 percent) among all main grocery buyers and buyers of breakfast cereals

who had seen the Event.   Growth rates in Past-Four-Week-Purchase was noted with +138.9 percent for Sustain; 84.7 percent for Special K; 74.6 percent for Sultana Bran. No product's growth in sales among those seeing the Event fell below +41 percent.   Increase in advertising awareness also occurred; Just Right +24.5 percent; Sultana Bran +111.2 percent; Special K +69.8 percent."
AGB.

Client: Quaker Trading
Brand: Quick & Hearty
Category: Hot breakfast Cereals
Country: UK
Year: 1994
Research by: NOP

North West England:
"Of those who only saw the television commercial one percent claimed to have purchased Quick and Hearty in the past four weeks, whilst those who had seen the interactive programmed nine percent claimed to have purchased, an increase of +800 percent."

In London:
"There was no television advertising for Quick & Hearty, the purchase of Quick & Hearty in the control area was 0 percent whilst in the interactive test area last four weeks purchase was four percent and increase of +700 percent"

In both regions:
"[the]... programme generated a nine percent positive intention to purchase.   This was twice the level generated in the North West and Midlands, and over three times that of the non advertising area in London. It is therefore a reasonable conclusion that the booklet led to an enhanced interest in purchasing Quick & Hearty when next buying a breakfast cereal."
NOP

Client: British Airways.
Brand: British Airways.
Category: Airline Flight.
Country: UK
Year: 2003
Research: City Insights.

"Airline Last Used has increased from 67 percent to 77 percent. Always choose to fly with BA and recommend to friend and colleagues increases from 24% to 31 percent. Increase in those saying BA has the best Frequent Flyer programme increases from 47 percent to 58 percent."

City Insights

Client: Reckitt & Colman.
Brand: Setamol 500
Category: Analgesic
Country: Australia
Year: 1984
Research: AGB

"Findings from this Post Event Survey shows impressive increases in scores for those who saw the Event in comparison for those who did not. Results are consistently superior in all three key market measures: Prompted-Brand-Awareness +92.6 percent, Past-Four-Week-Purchase +47 percent and Definitely-Will-Buy +47 percent."

AGB.

Client: Warner Lambert.
Brand: Listerine.
Product Category: Mouthwash
Country: Japan
Year: 1989
Research: Market Intelligence Corporation.

"Gains in all key measurements were recorded among consumers exposed to the newspaper interactive event, versus those not exposed. These gains were: Unaided Awareness 39 percent, Aided 11 percent, Past-Four-Week-Purchase 55 percent and Next-Purchase 97 percent. This translates in total market gain of eight percent for Unaided-Awareness; two percent gain in Aided-Awareness; 11 percent increase in Past-Four-Weeks-Purchase and 19 percent in Brand-Next-Purchase."

Market Intelligence Corporation.

Client: Warner Lambert.
Brand: Listerine.
In-Store Sampling Programme
Country: Japan
Year: 1986
Research: Market Intelligence Corporation.

"Research Protocol: interactive sampling was conducted in six stores with other six matched stores used as a control group where sampling was conducted without the interactive elements. Additionally, other stores that had no sampling programme at all were monitored. Purchase behaviour was monitored for three months. Actual inventory and cases sold were monitored.

"For the month of November (time of sampling and commencement of survey) an increase of 129 percent in actual purchase was obtained in those stores where the interactive sampling programme took place versus those (control) stores where the interactive sampling did not take place.

"The average for the three month programme, November, December, January, was a gain of 36 percent in purchase, versus those stores where the interactive programme was not held."

Market Intelligence Corporation.

Client: Nestle
Brand: Nescafe Excella Coffee
Product: Instant Coffee
Country: Japan
Year: 1985
Research: Market Intelligence Corporation

"Substantial gains in all key measurements were recorded among those readers who were exposed to the interactive event versus those who were not. Unaided Awareness of the brand increased 19 percent; Aided-Awareness increased 10 percent; Past-Four-Week-Purchase increased 33 percent and Brand-Next-Likely increased 31 percent. In the total market these increases translated to a four percent increase in Unaided-Awareness; two percent increase in Aided-Awareness; eight percent increase in Past-Four-Week Purchase and eight percent increase in Future Purchase-Intent.

"Follow-up programme in same publications seven months after above programme.

"As a result of the feedback from the above programme, the creative was strengthened to focus on a secondary feature of the above. OpinionGram responses from this programme event suggested this repositioning.

"Increases in all key measurements were recorded: Unaided-Awareness + 60 percent; Aided-Awareness + eight percent; Past-Four-Week-Purchase +70 percent and Next-Brand-Purchase +54 percent.

"The effect on the total market among those exposed versus not exposed was in the magnitude of: Unaided-Awareness +12 percent; Aided-Awareness + two percent; Past-Four-Week-Purchase +15 percent and Brand-Will-Buy-Next =11 percent."

Market Intelligence Corporation

Client: Nestle
Brand: Maggi Pantry Classics (non-frozen RTE meals)
Country: Australia
Year: 1985
Research: AGB

"There was an increase of 86.7 percent amongst those who saw the event in Prompted-Brand-Awareness versus those who didn't see. On Past-Four-Week-Purchase there was an increase of 233.3 percent and 266.7 percent increase in Future-Purchase-Intent (DWB) amongst those people who saw the event."
AGB

Client: Chesebrough-Pond's
Brand: Intensive Care Hand & Nail Lotion
Country: USA
Year: 1987
Research: Burke Market Research

"Readers of the event were significantly more likely than non-readers to re-call all four copy points, additionally readers were significantly more likely than non-readers to have tried the lotion, to have repeated buying it and to have purchased the brand recently.
Burke Market Research

Client: Rexona (Unilever)
Brand: Vaseline Intensive Care
Country: USA
Year: 1987
Research: AGB

"Prompted-Brand-Product-Awareness increased at the rate of 31.5 percent among people seeing the event, similarly and increase in Past-Four-Week-Purchase +90 percent and in increase of 81.8 percent Definitely-Will-Buy was recorded."
AGB

Consumers are suspicious

Research published recently by Beyond Philosophy in 1989, a UK company specialising in customer attitudes, claimed 82 percent of people never believe their experience of an organisation will match the image promoted by television advertising. Beyond Philosophy concluded television advertising may actually be harming, rather than enhancing, the relationships between companies and their customers.

Similarly, research by the Henley Centre in 1999 has shown while nine out of 10 people will trust their spouse or partner and eight out of 10 their children, fewer than a third (27 percent) trust retailers or manufacturers, while just 14 percent trust either the Government or advertisers.

And here is our Government, the largest advertiser by far, hiring advertising agencies to prepare information the majority of the nation increasingly distrusts. Shouldn't someone be telling them this is an unacceptable waste of taxpayer's money? The Enron collapse and the circumstances behind it are nothing compared to the waste and misuse of monies which has been fostered by the advertising industry.

So, how have we come to this state? Perhaps it all started as stores and communities grew larger and the personal bonds of trust and loyalty which used to be enjoyed by the local trader, who knew his customers wants and needs, disappeared.

In today's marketplace, time, attention and trust seem to have become the scarcest resources and companies who fail to recognise this fact are bound to suffer problems. As a result, it is becoming more and more important to ensure there is a strong 'what's in it for me' appeal to the consumer. With so many demands on their time, they will only spend quality time with those products and services which are clearly offering them something of direct personal relevance and value.

Another contributor to the loss of trust and belief has been the acceptance of the 'mass market'. Anyone with any understanding of communication and human behaviour will understand there has never been such a thing as a mass market. Buying habits are as individual as fingerprints, so the surest way to identify products and services of greatest appeal is not through traditional market segmentation and then advertising, but by a means of involving the customer in the process whereby a true two-way dialogue can be entered into. By analysing response from such 'events' i.e. by listening to the customer, it is possible to target commercial messages based on what has been learnt, that are relevant to those customers and which they will be prepared to listen to. Taking the process a step further, manufacturers and service providers can take the lessons learned from the feedback of their customers and develop the products and services themselves, which customers have expressed they want.

I often ask myself why I seem to be a lone voice in championing customer involvement and interaction. After all, anyone with a modicum of understanding must surely see the logic, mustn't they? So, why is there such a blind spot for those involved in conventional, award winning advertising? Perhaps because the perfect model for the advertising executive of today is Christopher Columbus. Consider these facts. He set off with no clear idea of where he was going. When he arrived he didn't know where he was. When he returned he didn't know where he had been. And he did it all on other peoples' money. Sound familiar?

Over the past decade, a consensus has formed among researchers that the power of television commercials to affect sales ranges from the insignificant to the non-existent. Some of the most acclaimed and memorable ads of all times have been pretty awful at doing what they were created for i.e. selling products. They look good and yes, viewers enjoy them, sometimes more than the programme content. But did it make them buy the product?

Here's what Kate Bruges, the Marketing Director of J Walter Thompson, said in 2001: "The conventional stuff won't ever go away. An awful lot of this unconventional stuff is the icing on the cake, that extra bit of media mileage. But it's never going to give you the cost-efficient mileage or get the message across consistently enough to a large enough number of people."

I believe there are better ways of communicating with consumers than 'conventional stuff'. It is fascinating she talks about cost efficiency. In my opinion her methods are not as cost effective as those I advocate.

It's a bit like Free Standing Inserts (FSIs) in the US, which are a collection of full colour coupon pages, distributed as newspaper inserts. The misuse of these coupons has always been a concern to manufacturers as they are the closest thing to cash. Consequently, even organised crime has literally cashed in and 'managed' the racket of sending in the coupons for payment, when no actual product to allow the coupon value against, has been purchased. One client is on record as saying: "They (FSIs) are like a roller- coaster. You desperately want to get off but are too frightened to do so." Can we draw an analogy with the client's view of advertising? Is the rollercoaster of reliance on the myth of 'conventional stuff' going so fast there is a fear of getting off and trying something else?

Well, there are many clients who are at least making some attempt to disengage from what has been fed to them for all these years and with good reason. The first rule of advertising, obviously, is to get noticed, but this is easier said than done. In the advertising arena everyone is trying to get noticed, and this results in clutter. When every adult person is bombarded with millions of advertising messages a year, yes millions, to acknowledge and act upon even a small proportion of these messages is a huge call on our time. And time is the one irreplaceable commodity more and more of us are guarding jealously.

Many clients, therefore, have started to question traditional advertising approaches and the traditional media which support them. Not least because buying time and space in traditional media is expensive. Particularly as the number of channels of communication (television channels, magazines) grow, the clutter affect grows too.

The result? Agencies will try to up the ante, producing more and more unusual, surprising and in some instances, shocking advertising. As "uninvited guests" into our homes, however, advertisements can only push the boundaries of shock and surprise as far as the industry regulators allow.

Mega-advertisers simply go for broke and outspend their competition. The downside of this is familiarity can breed, if not contempt, then certainly, irritation. Will that make people buy?

Some advertisers are gravitating towards PR, of which guerrilla marketing is an offshoot. This seeks to get people to notice a product or service by way of a newsworthy event. Most advocates of guerrilla marketing are really believers in what is now known as media neutrality. While many advertising agencies are still saying: "The answer is a 30-second television commercial, now what is the question?" But, as they fiddle on, the real world increasingly requires more radical and creative solutions.

Here are some approaches that certainly made an impact.

In 1880, Buchanans, the forerunner of Distillers, wanted to promote whisky in brandy-loving London. It hired 12 young men to go to the Ritz and order the drink. When the barman confessed he had none, they burst into laughter and proclaimed loudly: "The Ritz hasn't got Buchanans." They did the same thing in other top hotels. The taste soon caught on.

On Easter Sunday 1929, the makers of Lucky Strike staged a "debutantes march" in Fifth Avenue in New York. The women called the cigarettes "torches of freedom" and claimed it was a march for equality. It made front-page news, and prompted a debate about women and smoking.

Two male streakers pulled off a publicity coup for Vodafone during a rugby union clash between Australia and New Zealand in August 2002. They were arrested and the mobile phone company was threatened with prosecution for complicity. Sydney police called the stunt a "bad advertisement" for rugby. But even I am now referring to the brand in the context of this stunt, demonstrating its affect years later.

Tourists in New York were approached by good-looking people who wanted their picture taken with their new Sony Ericsson mobile phone. The Japanese-Swedish company had in fact hired 60 actors as part of a £3m project to convince passers-by the gadget was the new hip thing but provoked fierce criticism from rival marketers.

During the football World Cup in 2002, Nike spent a reported £10m on its "Scorpion" campaign. A football tournament for children was held at the Millennium Dome in London and electronic adverts on the sides of buses showed the latest World Cup scores. A survey found more people thought Nike rather than Adidas was the official World Cup sponsor.

TheStreet.com, a financial news company, sent specially branded luggage through carousels at Atlanta airport in spring 2002. It also hired actors to dress as chauffeurs and hold signs reading "The Street.com for Bill Gates".

Interacting with the audience, rather than the one-way message sending of the 30-second TV spot, creates measurable results.

Communication in a changing world

The advertising, marketing and broadcast community currently resides in a tramline society, a society which has got used to its ruts and its blinkers and prefers its own ways, however dreary, to untrodden paths and new ways of looking at things. An analogous story is of the Peruvian Indians who, seeing the sails of their Spanish invaders on the horizon, simply put it down to a freak in the weather and went on about their business having no concept of sailing ships in their limited experience. Likewise, advertising agencies lack understanding of the communication process. Similarly they pay only lip service to the much-needed concept of accountability.

The huge changes about to engulf this community need not be painful, however, these changes are inevitable because the old ways of marketing and advertising have gone forever. They have been exposed as having failed the needs of the whole community.

Marketing applies advertising to the selling of goods or services, so, what is advertising? It is nothing more than a form of learning. The advertiser is simply saying to his audience: "Learn about my product/service and then please change or modify your behaviour."

Well then, what is learning?

Most educationalists today say real learning is about answering a question or solving a problem. The questions can range from the immense to the trivial, however, when we have no questions we need no answers. Apply questions and an understanding of human behaviour to the marketing of products, then you start to have real communication taking place.

The questions do not have to be some kind of examination question, more often it is a sort of reaching for, an exploration. Learning is a discovery and people do want to learn about and discover products.

As I said earlier on, you cannot expect the consciousness which created the problem to then solve the problem. Advertising and marketing people spend hours and hours at conferences discussing the latest whiz in marketing and indulging in Group Think. A most dangerous past time because like-minded groups have like-minded ideas and find it hard among themselves to project change in their profession, any meaningful change that is.

Study the English marketing trade press, one would think all was safe and calm within their industry, they constantly discuss the latest multi-million dollar advertising (waste of money) and how it fares creatively. The current account changes and, all the while, never giving any indication theirs is a profession undergoing critical examination and the verdict is almost upon them: death of a thousand cuts.

Forget Enron

As you will already have ascertained, it is my view current, conventional mass media advertising has been beset with problems from the very beginnings. Probably the principal problem advertising has is accountability. Or rather the lack of it.

As we have said before, the real differences which exist between competing products is frequently perceived as no longer significant.

The result is that it is not self evident just what an advertiser has to sell which is so different and worthy of consideration.

Therefore, if no significant point of difference is apparent, why is this product more deserving of the customer's money than any other?

It was partially because of this we have seen a dramatic rise in the acceptance of own-label products and now services, in this country as elsewhere.

Tesco, Sainsbury's, Asda and so on, all developed their own-label offerings and the manufacturers, along with their agencies observing on the sidelines, sat back and let them do it.

In some cases they were complicit in doing so.

Now own-label has become so acceptable to consumers that they not only cover grocery products and, with a differentiation between value and premium, the brand extensions encompass, motor insurance, home insurance, life cover and a multitude of offers which did not exist only a few years ago.

It is interesting to note we are now subjected to messages which not only extol the virtues of branded products, they even go so far as to make a point that certain companies do not make own-label, to justify their premium pricing.

You have to take your hat off to the ad man who came up with the little gem of building a campaign out of that one.

Sadly, for the client, the horse had already bolted. But the ad men, as usual, were pocketing their fees and laughing all the way to the bank.

It is no surprise then, with more and more competition, now including own label, there has been a significant increase in the number of advertisements, vying for customers' attention. So, with more competition in the marketplace and more competition to attract the viewer/reader to engage with the message, what's the solution?

"We don't show many clients this…" is a statement we have actually heard in the agency environment, and didn't we all think that agencies were a service industry there to tell their clients everything in their best interests.

Here is an example of what they are not telling. It is from America but we see no reason why it should be any different in any marketplace. The research, conducted in 2002 questioned whether the expensively produced advertisements shown on television were actually getting anywhere.

The figures began with the average numbers of hours Americans watch television each week: 47.

This consisted then, of 43.5 hours of network, local independent or cable television, two and three-quarter hours of playback of recorded video, and 50 minutes of pre-recorded rented or purchased video.

Those figures applied to the average home in the average week.

Out of that time, television provided seven-and-a-half hours of commercials however, because of zapping, or people talking or going to the bathroom, and all the other things that people choose to do when the commercials come on, the seven-and-a-half hours falls to one hour, 27 minutes of commercials actually seen.

Translated, this means each individual sees about 120 television advertisements a week. The networks average about 4,000 commercials a week.

So, let's emphasise what this really means for advertisers, because these are true figures which demonstrate why the advertising industry waste is bigger than Enron, only 120 advertisements are seen each week by the average viewer.

Is this an isolated piece of research? If only.

The Royal Mail in the UK commissioned research in 2004 which produced a similar picture. It showed more than a quarter of the people who had watched an edition of *News at Ten* had seen none of the commercials. Great news? Not so. Of the remaining 75 percent, 26 percent simply hadn't paid attention, 21 percent had made a drink, 20 percent left the room, 11 percent were preoccupied with other things, eight percent switched channel, six percent went to the bathroom and five percent talked to someone.

It is clear from the likes of the above, that television advertising is not seen by many of the audience out there.

However, the advertising industry tries to get around this by quoting reach and frequency.

OK, not everyone views at the same time, but run enough ads and this will counter this. Does this really hold true?

As I have already discussed, the majority of the ads which are 'seen' very often, never 'break through'.

The human mind cannot give weight to everything which comes its way; the brain decides not to bother with most ads at all, or, if it does, it rapidly forgets them.

It is estimated by many different sources, that in 2001 every adult in this country was subjected to 3,000 advertising messages every day. Now talk is of in excess of 8,000. [*Media Week, Campaign, Marketing Week.*]

To add to the horror of it all, it is estimated only about one-third of those commercials a person is exposed to, make any active impression in the memory. Of those which make any impact, only about half are correctly comprehended and fewer than five percent are actively recalled for as long as 24 hours.

And we thought Enron was the biggest business scandal ever.

Yet, despite all the evidence, when you talk to advertising people they constantly repeat the yet, unproved, mantra: "Advertising increases sales." Yes, of course, there have been advertising campaigns which have produced sales, given the fact there are billions (dollars, pounds, yen, you make the choice) spent every year, there have to be one or two which produce results.

However, shouldn't we be asking, given the fact advertising exists in perilous times these days, why hasn't the industry yet produced the definitive piece of research which finally, conclusively, once and for all, proves advertising makes the difference which merits the ever-inflating cost?

You could say they do try but do they really? An article in the 21st November 2001 issue of *Marketing* in the UK, alerted us to new research commissioned by ITV, which it says, proves television to be the most powerful communication medium. Oh really? But wait, here comes the earth-shattering bit. The study showed the brain finds audio visual images easier to process than either text or audio alone. (Hands up everyone who can see where this is going.)

An article in The Times in 2002 explained how Professor of Psychology at Manchester University, Geoffrey Beatie, exposed participants to three (yes three) products, a holiday, a car and a mobile phone, via an audio visual message (video), an audio message and a text message. Retention and recall were much stronger from audio visual. Aren't we all amazed? Not as amazed as the statement from ITV's marketing director that this "is the most important piece of ad hoc research ITV has undertaken." Ad hoc, so just what is the purpose? To show viewers watch ads or is it an attempt to say television works better than radio? Well you might think marketing believes this to be the case as they elicit a response from The Radio Advertising Bureau: "The ad avoidance issue is a significant one for television," (can't fault them so far) "an Initiative study shows 44 percent of viewers actively avoid ads on television. It is only 16 percent for radio." So, there it is, no further forward after all. No conclusive evidence that TV advertising produces results. However, what do you think, is this a good example of two rivals trying to knock each other?

But, still no research showing advertising works and shouldn't we also be asking why the television business hasn't produced a similar study which proves, once and for all, television advertising produces results consistently?

One would have thought that the advertising industry and the terrestrial television business would have worked hand-in-glove to answer the £64,000 question: "Does television advertising pay off?

The various systems which do allow measurement scare the living daylights out of advertising people. The implications and the possibilities of these systems verge on the frightening. So much so, the people who create the commercials naturally start seeking excuses for not reading too much into such measurements.
"We may become so fixated in the ups and downs of transient share change we will not even think about the possibility what is being done today may have delayed effect and cumulative effects next week, next month, maybe even next year." Wow. If only advertising was as good as this, but as usual, it's all spin and no substance.

I remember when I first entered the advertising business, I was so in awe of my more experienced colleagues, they knew the holy grail, they knew secrets I didn't, they knew the words and images which sold millions of products to unsuspecting consumers. I vowed to learn all I could from these incredible people but the longer I stayed in advertising, the more I learnt one thing, these people knew nothing. The whole thing was a charade. No, more than that, it was and still is, one big gigantic confidence trick which literally puts Enron to shame.

"How could this be," I have often wondered.

Well, advertising has attracted more than its fair share of comments. These, in turn, have led to an assessment of advertising which substantially misinformed us as to the power of advertising to change attitudes and sell products or services.

It also produced a highly insulting attitude towards the very people to whom they, the advertising industry, wanted to sell to, the long-suffering consumer.

The industry really believed they could almost inject anything into the mass communication process and have the majority of people behave the way they wanted them to.

Well, thank goodness, the majority of the population has far greater sense than they are given credit for, they know they are being pitched to, usually in a highly unsatisfactory way.

When I explained I was contemplating a career in advertising, one of my professors cried out in dismay: "But it's so amoral."

In a major article, "Commercial Breakdown", The *Financial Times* in 1998 said "...as questions about the effectiveness of mass marketing have grown, advertising has been assailed by other doubts too. Where once it was thought that commercials sold goods and increased brand awareness, it is now acknowledged that many of them do no such thing: most people never actually buy the majority of products they see advertised on television."

There was a time when admen were proud to be admen. From their horn-rimmed spectacles and flashy braces right down to the austere name on the sand blasted glass of their terribly fashionable Soho offices. Not any more it seems.

In 2003, another agency opened its doors in London. However, there is one major difference, the people working in this new agency don't like being called an advertising agency, they prefer 'brand communication company'.

They are far from alone. Increasingly the 'A' word is not mentioned at the best media parties. Suggest to someone they are in advertising and you can expect a long explanation about why they are not. The buzzword instead is 'media neutral', which tells a client to expect a range of solutions including public relations, marketing, product development and, from some quarters I have heard, starting rumours on the internet.

Long regarded as the ultimate weapon in the marketing armoury, conventional advertising, particularly the once-mighty television commercial, is now seen as complacent and increasingly ineffective.

The real problem may be our entire system of valuing advertising is completely screwed up. In every major medium, the basic benchmark for pricing ads is. Cost Per Thousand (CPT).

Is conventional advertising really dead? It sure seems that way. There has been a proliferation of articles bemoaning the ineffectivess of advertising. More and more, people assiduously avoid ads in consumer magazines, they are turning away in droves from commercial television or have access to technology which can fast-forward through commercials. More broadly though, there's a sense technology is in the process of killing mass market advertising.

`When you look at the sums involved, however, especially in America, it would seem advertising is certainly not dead. In the USA radio advertising still generates more than $15 billion a year, magazine advertising about $12 billion and television $35 billion.

But, here's where it gets interesting, can anyone say for sure any of these: television, radio, magazines, etc, are reliable indicators of the real cost of advertising? I don't think so. The supposedly reliable benchmarks of those media were actually, mutually agreed upon illusions. No company expects that, by paying a magazine £40 for each thousand subscribers, it will actually get all those people to read its ad.

If advertising isn't dead, then the way we measure its value is going to need to be radically different in the future.

Yet, despite all the evidence, clients will continue to delude themselves and close their eyes and ears to what their customers are really seeking. Following a presentation and follow-up I did, a reply was received from the Director of Marketing Consumer Division: "At present we have no plans to introduce a product as yours (ignore the grammar) (sic) into our marketing programme." Why? Because what they are doing already is so good. So good in fact they keep sending direct mail pieces to my mother who died some time ago, despite being repeatedly told she is no longer with us. If this one example is anything to go by, they must surely be shedding customers at a dramatic rate and the share price of the company may soon drop from pounds to pennies. His response to me concluded they: will keep your letter and presentation on file, should circumstances change." Who is deluding who?

Not all clients think the same way. In 2001 Quaker Oats had this to say, "Television still delivers high quality broadcast messages and we continue to use it but not in isolation. We have employed direct mail, door drops, web-based promotions, sponsorship and sampling to ensure the headlines of the television activity are fleshed out with more direct product experience and product specific communications."

Marvellous. All we need are for more clients to move forward in this way and true interactive communication between manufacturer and consumer will become common place.

Who's running your organisation?

Your customers, that's who.

Or should be.

Don't you think that you ought to start a regular dialogue with them?

The word empowerment is a very overused word. However, in the near future the primary strategic marketing communication battle will be to see who goes furthest in empowering their customers.

To empower your customers you will have to:

1 Provide them with far more information than you currently do

2 Allow them to make decisions about you and your company together with your resources

3 Give them plenty of choice

4 Give them the perception of control

5 Allow them to feel they are running your organisation.

Anything which tightens your relationships with an existing customer increases the revenue you get from your customer.

And the only form of communication which can do all the above so you do tighten your grip on your customer is interactive communication.

Interactive communication allows you to have an ongoing debate with your customers and your prospects, make regular interactive conversations available where they can debate, not only your products and services, but the very soul of your company. Because that will be much more powerful than just putting your advertisement on television (or wherever) or I'm going to sell my goods in Tesco (or wherever).

Then, when you get asked: "Who's running your business?" you can honestly reply: "My customers through genuine interactive programmes," and earn major brownie points.

Because the problems with the current system are manifest. The challenges faced by marketing and advertising stem largely from the institutional dimensions of both. Remove these old models from the equation and many of the existing problems of lack of sales, etc, will disappear.

Nowadays, consumers want information which is relevant, credible and engaging, and they don't much care where it comes from.

The subject of interactive communication has been the focus of innumerable articles in the popular press. Most of these have looked at the phenomenon through a mass media lens, with "interactivity" reduced to advertising links and "buy-it" buttons.

And certainly not understanding the very important fact interactivity is the most crucial aspect of all communication. And it is certainly not determined by the expectations of media conglomerates bent on appealing to the lowest common denominator and therefore, by the inexorable and inflexible logic of broadcast, to the largest collection of passive ad receivers.

Today, consumers don't like ad-infested terrestrial television. What they do like is the opportunity to express an opinion, what they like, in other words, is a voice.

So, just who is running your organisation?

One bit of advice, for goodness sake, don't let your advertising agency have a say in that running. The only running you should be doing in that instance is away... as fast as you can.

Advertising agencies who constantly stay attuned to their target audience are confronted again and again by the market's diversity. As a consequence, they assume markets almost always must be segmented with strategies fine-tuned to the needs and wants of each sub-population.

Closeness to consumers also leads to the recognition traditional demographic approaches are seldom adequate to capture the rich diversity in target audience's needs, wants, life-styles, perceptions and preferences.

Getting in sync with this massive transformation of marketing is not going to be easy. The problem is, our minds are conditioned by the past, not the future. So we want to keep doing things the way we have always done them, even when the results become ever more disappointing.

Every now and then the ground beneath us shifts so dramatically as to make much of what we thought we knew so wrong it becomes clear we have to forge new beliefs or fail.

These are such times in marketing. The behavioural proclivities of consumers as individuals must be the primary determining factor, not exotic maths even though it will obviously continue to be a critical tool, but not the main tool.

That is why it essential to fully understand and comprehend the meaning of the word communication. To interact is to communicate, all else is a sheer waste of time, energy and money. Your money.

Let us recall the essential elements of business, and especially advertising and marketing-as-usual, in the 20th century. Mass production and its attendant economies of scales exemplified business for most of the past 100 years.

Perhaps the reason for this hanging on to the past way of doing things is the persistence of mass media, which came about as a result of the needs of business as a way of reaching mass markets.

Like the management of large corporations, broadcast advertising partakes of the same top-down style of command and control.

Customers were told what to do, shop hard, but not asked in any substantive way for their input or opinions.

And, sad to say, command and control remains the order of the day. There is much talk these days about the empowerment of consumers, although corporations still communicate their demands by broadcasting them to demographically determined abstractions, of whom they know very little about, and have no genuine relations with at all.

When it comes to change, when it comes to improving methods of communicating with customers, both mainstream media and corporate marketing are blind to these changes in as much as they continue to rely on deep seated assumptions attached to advertising-as-usual.

When we dared to challenge the obvious assumptions of advertising-as-usual and its unshakeable supremacy of the 'creative' solution to marketing-as-usual, we were considered, in a word: nuts.

In fact, we were regarded as demented, deranged, and certainly totally unaware as to the unassailable supremacy of the advertising-as-usual model.

What happens when the great masters of the universe, broadcast media and their lackeys, advertising agencies, have to confront the fact they are about to be made redundant, superfluous, by a far superior technique, interaction.

Well, these corporations are finally discovering advertising-as-usual is exorbitantly expensive and it is a ridiculously inefficient means of trying to reach and form productive relationships with an increasingly fragmented array of markets.

And, the scary thing for advertising-as-usual is corporations don't give one damn about advertising. All they want is the best, most efficient way of getting their goods to market and sold. The day of advertising-as-usual is gone.

Off to see the Wizard

Let us review something written and published in *Marketing* magazine in 2004. The author is Marc Ritson, Assistant Professor of Marketing at The London Business School.

"A pipe bursts in your house. When the local handyman arrives, he is carrying a large toolbox.

"Without even looking at the pipe, he opens the box to reveal only one tool: a hammer. He takes it out and brings it crashing down on the broken pipe - for an hour. With the pipe destroyed, he asks for £100 and leaves."

This provides an accurate analogy for the state of the marketing communication industry.

The fanfare which greeted the emergence of integrated marketing communications in the early 1990s has long died away, leaving the industry uncomfortably aware that it still represents a series of one-trick ponies.

Advertising agencies still espouse solutions which centre on advertising.

PR agencies always suggest PR; direct agencies suggest direct marketing and so on.

Like our handyman, each fails to diagnose the problem correctly and opts to solve all their clients' communication issues with one tool.

Ask WPP chief executive Sir Martin Sorrell. He recently bemoaned the fact most agencies 'redefine every problem in terms of their proposed solution.'

As Sir Martin knows, different communication tools have different strengths.

This has two implications. First, a company must completely diagnose the communication challenge before it assigns the communication tools to be used in its strategy.

For many clients, tools such as advertising, PR or sponsorship, will prove entirely ineffective no matter how well they are applied because they are wrong tool for the job.

Secondly, by combining two or more communication tools into an integrated campaign, a company is likely to realise significant synergies.

An integrated strategy, which spreads its budget across a combination of PR, direct marketing and event marketing, is pretty much guaranteed to have a greater impact than a campaign opting to spend the total budget on just one of them.

The ideal model is obvious: a handyman with a variety of tools, who first studies the problem, then selects a combination of tools to solve the problem.

But, this model has proved impossible to replicate in marketing communication terms. Despite owning an impressive list of different organisations which represent every major communication tools, WPP, for example, has consistently failed, in my opinion, to get its organisations to work together for their clients' common good.

Even within the structures of WPP, the concept of an integrated campaign in which BPRI Group does the research, Added Value positions the brand, Landor designs the new corporate identity, Y & R does the media advertising, Burson-Marsteller does the PR and Ogilvy Direct runs the customer relationship management strategy, remains a pipe dream.

Integration on the supply side it seems, will never occur.

Turf wars, egos and a lack of common systems and understanding means agencies will remain segregated. The only potential site of integration resides on the demand side with the client. It is up to clients to diagnose their problems, select and motivate these groups to work in a single strategic agenda.

Unfortunately, clients with these skills, power and confidence to achieve this are thin on the ground (they seek 'expert' agencies for a reason). For now, integration will remain the Holy Grail of marketing.

In 1776, Thomas Paine wrote in *Common Sense*: "We have it in our power to begin the world over again. A situation, similar to the present hath not happened since the days of Noah until now."

In the same year, the American Revolution and the building of that New World was underway.

Still, more or less still on the threshold of this new millennium, interactive communication has given us the power to build a New World.

But, as in Thomas Paine's time, most have yet to grasp how different the newly forming world will be from the world which is passing. And many are aware are afraid to embrace it, being so steeped in the status quo. and used to working only with hammers.

We stand wide-eyed at the portal of another New World. Some of us, fearful of what is to be, look backward, pining for a simplicity that in reality we probably never experienced.

Others may be more like Dorothy who, after being cyclonically blown away from the greyness of Kansas, suddenly found herself standing in wide-eyed wonderment amid the colourful splendour and magic of Oz.

We may be tentative as Dorothy was; not quite sure of the meaning of all we see in this New World, but we are ready to move on. We want to see what the Wizard of Interaction has in store for us.

There is plenty of evidence as to the interactive wonders available to us right now.

On the cost effectiveness of just one exposure to my interactive programme, Professor E L Roberto, PhD, Coca-Cola Foundation Professor of International Marketing, had this to say after studying all the independent research: "The *Shopper's Voice* participating advertisements generated recall scores that are more than 50 percent more productive than normal advertising. The effect on purchase intention is just as impressive if not much more.

"All these productivity increments are attainable at a reasonably inexpensive budget. One *Shoppers' Voice* client revealed for its participating brand, its quarter television expenditure was $5.7 million as compared to its *Shopper's Voice* budget of $0.5 million. This 1:10 ratio has been experienced in *Shopper's Voice* in other countries."*

Many marketers seem unconcerned about the advent of interactive communication because they are not yet persuaded about the powerful benefits to be gained by using the technique despite the evidence.

Probably less concerned are research houses, however, the richness of personal information provided by consumers through the process of interaction will significantly depreciate the value of standard research.

Consumers have generally tolerated uninvited marketing messages as a somewhat necessary evil. It was a price which had to be paid for access to most broadcast and print media.

Interactive communication has laid down the foundation for changing this. Reminiscent of a Gary Larson cartoon, in which a deer peers at a hunter through the cross hairs of his own rifle, companies are becoming the target of consumers.

In this scenario, and with the aid of interaction, consumers will manage their own marketing relationships, not vendors or marketers.

And in such a scenario, when a consumer has no need of a company, company access to that consumer will be shut off. Interactive communication participants find it refreshing they can get information in ways which track the personal grammar of their views, values, needs and lifestyle.

However, before advertisers can start reaping the benefits of interactive advertising, they must rise to the creative challenge posed by interactive services.

Although the cultural shift being demanded of the notoriously conservative advertising industry is huge and represents one of the major obstacles the new media services will have to overcome, the new services do have one argument in their favour: they will eliminate waste.

They will reach targeted consumers and the commercial message can be immediately translated into a sales opportunity, or even a sale.

By giving the consumer the opportunity to respond directly to the advertiser, the role of agencies as an interface between the advertiser and the customer will decline and a new productive age will have dawned.

* Sources: AGB: Gallup: Martyn Research: Bourke: NOP. City Insights and others in tests conducted between 1979-2005.

Understanding interactive marketing communication

Interaction can be defined simply as straightforward communication between two parties. Presently we are in danger of losing the real meaning of interaction as we tend to focus discussions on the emerging technologies and neglect the communication process itself. With an understanding of the real meaning of interactive communication, existing media can be made interactive, and subsequently far more cost effective.

Goodbye to the halcyon days of the television advertisement of old?

A new wave of technology is transforming the obsolete analogue technology of television into a two-way medium which allows the viewer to determine what is to be watched, and when.

This could well create a situation where the consumers solicit information from the advertiser, rather than the advertiser soliciting the attention of the consumer.

Viewers are becoming impatient with television's linear flow and are increasingly using the opportunities available to them to avoid the intentions of advertisers and programme makers. Even though, to many, the remote control is a fairly recent development, 44 percent habitually use it to avoid advertisements.

Television is an advertising medium, not a communication medium and, as television declines in the face of competition from the new media, conventional advertising will decline with it.

In many ways, 'advertising' is an outmoded concept, since media advertising is simply one means of communication with customers. In an environment in which the balance of power is shifting in favour of the consumer rather than the advertiser, manufacturers and service providers need to look at ways of replacing the monologue of advertising with a dialogue which can utilise a range of different 'relationship' marketing techniques.

Advertising has to modernise and change.

The market place has changed. Newspapers and television have lost their exclusive hold on the advertiser, the number of print and electronic advertising channels has substantially increased, such as local cable television, direct mail and pre-printed booklets pushed through letterboxes, or hung on doorknobs.

Recent events have given advertising a permanently diminished role in the selling of goods and services. At the same, time cynical consumers are wearying of the constant barrage of marketing messages. They're becoming less receptive of the blandishments of advertisements, and their loyalty to brands erodes as they see more products as commodities distinguished only by price.

Advertising ignores communication theory. As the mass media has matured, the behavioural dynamics of perception and interaction, which were not addressed by advertising agencies in the 1970s and '80s, during the explosive growth of advertising, have become critical to the redefinition of media and its role in marketing communication. With passive, one-way, forms of advertising such as media displays or television advertising, there is a certain degree of non-response.

Most advertising agencies lack the skills of communication, advertising messages are more carefully prepared than interpersonal communication and yet 'message' comprehension tends to be lower. Advertisements are more carefully prepared because gatekeepers (those who prepare and send out messages) are more cautious about what they say to large audiences than they are to audiences of one or a few. They check their facts more carefully and they prepare their syntax and vocabulary more precisely. And yet, because their audience contributes much less feedback, the source cannot correct for any lapse or understanding, so people are more likely to misinterpret what they hear or read over the mass media.

It is also important to note, just because mediated messages are more carefully prepared, they are not necessarily more accurate. Gatekeepers have a way of looking at the world based on personal beliefs or motivations. This 'world view' sometimes tends to make media messages inaccurate.

However, with interactive marketing communication, there is a commitment to participate, which in turn leads to a set of possibilities, which are significantly different in how they affect the communication process itself.

Image advertising doesn't give the information needed to buy knowledge-driven products. Moreover, communication results from an interaction in which two parties expect to give and take. Audience members must be able to give feedback. Media practitioners must be sensitive to the information contained in the feedback. This give and take can result in real understanding or real feedback.

Put simply, because there is a human desire for interaction, we have created a media society during the past 40 or 50 years where there is an extraordinary reduction in interaction because of the one-way and more passive form of information retrieval which exists.

People desire to be taken account of, to affect change, learn and personalise their relationships with their environment. There are a phenomenal number of reasons which cause people to interact which go far beyond just giving them things.

When people participate in interactive marketing communication they are told their efforts and feedback are of positive help to the advertisers. Moreover, by participating, they then learn and understand the message from the advertiser, personalise their relationship with the advertiser and their products (or services).

Consumers tend to filter out information they do not want to hear and this alters the effectiveness of advertising in quite a dramatic way. The purchaser's decision is invariably a compromise and this leads to a certain amount of anxiety. The worry is perhaps the purchase decision was not the best or right one. In order to minimise this anxiety, the purchaser seeks to reinforce his choice and begins to take more notice of his chosen product's advertising. And, at the same time, the purchaser deliberately suppresses data that might challenge his decision by ignoring the advertising of competitive brands.

People are often loyal to a brand simply because they do not want to read-dress a decision. The opportunity to screen out undesired data always exists when media advertisements have to stand on their own and fight for attention.

Interactive communication takes the consumer through the barrier of not wanting to address change; and this is the ultimate market the advertiser is after: the people who use his competitors' products.

Now the consumer can say: "Yes, I will change my behaviour and I have a very good reason or series of reasons why," and have a well-informed opinion or im-age in mind.

If someone goes into a product purchase decision with a very specific im-age of the product and its reason to exist and why they have decided those reasons are worth its purchase, the test in reality, the use of the product, will tend to confirm that premise, and therefore conversion will be enormously enhanced.

Interactive marketing communication turns passive advertising into active advertising and actually alters behaviour during the communication and learning process.

And there's more.

It enhances relationships and dramatically improves consumer knowledge, understanding and loyalty.

1) Strong company or brand values

To be effective, communication has to be single-minded in choosing a spe-cific proposition which by definition cannot appeal to all. Yet, every product, service or retail outlet can offer several attractive benefits and, in some cases, these can be numerous. Interactive communication presents consumers with a 'menu' of power-ful benefits, both rational and emotional, and asks them to choose the one which they find most relevant and appealing to them.

This allows them:

• To personalise their relationship with the communicator.

• To absorb and retain the majority, or even all, of those extra benefits while making their choice

• Not one, but several, good reasons for buying the product or service.

Equally it puts these benefits into context, educating consumers to under-stand just how important those benefits are to them, and positions the product or service as unique in satisfying all those needs.

2) The emotional relationship

By asking consumers for their opinions rather than telling them, the com-pany makes them feel special and involved in an unprecedented way. A company prepared to listen. This disarms consumers and produces a feeling of trust and thereby an emotional commitment to the company and its products, which cannot be generated any other way.

This emotional commitment enhances the more rational understanding of the company or brand values discussed above and establishes an unprecedented, personal, relationship with the manufacturer/brand/retailer, even among those who may have had no previous experience.

3 Consumer feedback

Allowing consumers to interact with the brand by offering their opinions and views does more than create an emotional commitment; it allows large numbers of real people to express ideas in a way they have not had the facility to do before, to a company evidently prepared to listen and act.

Consumers are seduced and this generates genuinely expressed observations on the strengths of the company, as well as areas of opportunity for improvement or exploitation. It is, in effect, an enormous piece of qualitative research, but without consumers' ability to vouchsafe real opinions being inhibited or guided by a researcher.

Thus, the combination of all these elements produces a deep understanding of the company, its brands, as well as its role and value to the consumer; a greater level of involvement in an emotional commitment to the brand and an enhanced desire to buy it.

A better understanding of the nature of interaction allows us then to give a more precise definition of the process, which I define as:

"With interactive marketing communication the reader/viewer is actively encouraged to take careful note of what is being taught him, learn rather than be taught the message, and then give tangible evidence to the lesson, in this case the advertising/marketing message, has been learnt. Interactive marketing communication ensures the initial message receiver anticipates and then subsequently evidences a response using a predetermined mechanism."

The waning influence of advertising

The escalating cost and waning influence of advertising, in communicating to customers, is another factor in the inability to brand strongly and to sell goods.

"Mass advertising has lost its ability to move the masses," says Sergio Zyman, Coca-Cola's former marketing chief, in his book, *The End of Marketing as we Know it*. Technology has given people many more options than they had in the past and created a consumer democracy. Everybody has a thousand choices for any product they might want to buy and there are a million different products competing for our wallets. So marketers increasingly need to speak to customers individually, or in smaller and smaller groups.

But, are they really doing so or simply deluding themselves as usual and paying lip service to the idea?

As questions about the effectiveness of mass marketing have grown, advertising has been assailed by other doubts too. Where once it was thought commercials sold goods and increased brand awareness, it is now often acknowledged many of them do no such thing. Most people never actually buy the majority of products they see advertised on television.

But, if mass-market advertising does not sell products, what will?

The attraction of interactive communication is that it is a return to the prehistoric human fascination with telling tales.

Since the beginnings of any civilised society, the market place was the hub of civilisation, a place to which traders returned from remote lands with exotic spices, silks, monkeys, parrots, jewels and fabulous stories.

Interactive communication, properly executed, more resembles an ancient bazaar than it fits the business models companies try and impose upon it. People respond to interactive opportunities because it seems to offer some intangible quality long 'missing in action' from modern life. In sharp contrast to the alienation wrought by homogenised broadcast media, interactive opportunities provide a space in which the human voice would be rapidly rediscovered.

Unlike the lockstep conformity imposed by television, advertising, and corporate propaganda, interactive communication gives new legitimacy, and free rein, to play.

People long for more connection between what we do for a living and what we genuinely care about. We long for release from anonymity, to be seen as who we feel ourselves to be rather than the sum of abstract metrics and parameters. We long to be part of a world which makes sense rather than accept the accidental alienation imposed by market forces too large to grasp; to even contemplate.

Remember the market place, of old. Caravans arrived across burning deserts bringing dates and figs, snakes and parrots, monkeys, strange music and stranger tales. The market place was the heart of the city, the kernel, the hub. Like the past and the future it stood at the crossroads. People worked early and went there for coffee and vegetables, eggs and wine, for pots and carpets. They went there to look and listen and to marvel, to buy and to be amused. But, mostly, they went to meet each other, to talk and interact.

Markets are conversations.

So, what went so horribly wrong? From the perspective of corporations, many of which by the 20th century had become bigger and more powerful than ancient city-states, nothing went wrong. Things did change however.

Commerce is a natural part of human life but it has become increasingly unnatural over the intervening centuries, gradually divorcing itself from the very people on whom it depends, whether workers or customers. The result has been to create a huge chasm between buyers and sellers.

Conventional advertising has failed the natural human need for social interaction. We have created a media society during the last 40 or 50 years where there is an extraordinary reduction in interaction because of the one-way and more passive form of information which exists. People desire to be taken account of, to affect change, learn and personalise their relationships with their environment.

These psychological and sociological factors are part of the incentive to interact with advertising. However, these tend to be minimised in the incentive direct response field, there are a phenomenal number of reasons which cause people to interact which go beyond just giving them things.

With interactive advertising people are also told, in the copy, their efforts, their response, are of help to the advertisers. And, by completing their entry forms, the competitors, having understood and learned the message from the advertisers, personalise their relationships with the advertisers and their product.

As marketers, we are professional observers and communicators of our product's message. All the technology we use is nothing more than a set of tools. All the messages we produce are simply by-products (written, recorded or video taped) of what we hope has been a successful effort in telling others, many others, what is important about our products.

Ironically, when we think about or describe two people talking with each other, the focus is on two persons interacting. The view is a behavioural one, focused on human activities, not on the medium of communication or on the literal messages produced.

However, when we shift from the simplest form of communication, two people engaged in thoughtful conversation, to the more complex forms of mass communication, somehow our attention is distracted. We focus on the technologies interposed between the sender and the receiver and the sudden multiplication in the volume of messages despatched. These unfortunate distractions divert our attention from the essential elements of the communication process. While technology and multiple messages are necessary in mass communication they are far from sufficient for any actual communication to take place with the individual.

Communication results from an interaction in which two parties expect to give and take. Professional communicators, who ignore the characteristics and orientations of the audience members, do so at the peril of actual communication or information transmittal.

Put another way, mass communication, if it is to be successful, must take on many characteristics of interpersonal communication.

Audience members must be able to give feedback. In turn, media practitioners must be sensitive to the information contained in the feedback. This give and take is the lifeblood of successful communication.

So, okay what exactly is communication, considering how much we keep mentioning it?

Most people in media and advertising come up with a definition that communication is all about transmitting and receiving information. Think about it a little more and they might come up with the word 'exchange'. This is moving in the right direction, but still assumes communication is about moving something: about conveying, or sending, or delivering, something called 'information'.

In fact, the word has quite a different root meaning. It derives from the Latin 'communis', meaning 'common', or 'shared'. It belongs to the family of words which includes communion, communism and community. Until you have shared information with another person, you haven't communicated it. And until they have understood it, the way you understand it, you haven't shared it with them. Communication is the process of creating shared understanding.

With everything we have said about the failure of marketing-as-usual and advertising-as-usual, let us give you some advice. Firstly, loosen up a little and then start to listen, especially to your customer. Your are not fighting a war. They really do want to 'talk' to you and, in doing so, you'll start having some fun. But, most importantly, you'll start to really build a successful business not just for the present, the now, but for the future.

Now, to restate the obvious, the future of marketing is interactive.

Everything we have learned about the complicated process of communication leads us to one inescapable conclusion, the future is, no, has to be, interactive.

So much has to be done. Marketing departments must understand fully the benefits to be gained from applying interactive programmes and how to use such as a strategic tool. Marketing departments must learn to analyse and then affect the behaviour of consumers by creating dialogues between themselves, the sellers and their customers, the buyers and to build these dialogues into lasting relationships. It must make the home the new market place. It must increasingly, become personal, relevant, measurable and profitable, for all concerned.

The Industrial Revolution created the practice of branding but, in the New Information Age, brand images increasingly provide only a thin shield against competitors.

In the Industrial Age, advertisers and marketers long believed the product and brand were the centre of the world. Brand images and brand personalities were key items in the Industrial Age, a totally attitudinal concept which assumed attitude is the primary determinant of consumer behaviour.

Today, advertising is increasingly measured by harsher criteria. Many of the world's largest advertisers have demanded that their advertising be more directly accountable for sales.

The Interactive Age provides just that.

The Oscars – 2007

And the winner is? ABC television of course.

The network got roughly $1.7million per 30-second advertising spot during its exclusive broadcast of the awards. The total revenue of more than $80million is double what it was in 1998, despite the show's variable ratings.

Out there in the real world, the world where all these millions of dollars are spent, the world where we, the ordinary people who do not attend the awards ceremony, it emerges that only 57 percent of consumers are inclined to trust companies and resistance to marketing is also now at a peak. With just six percent of consumers admitting to trusting any form of advertising.

Communication, even within the Oscars awards ceremony, is not a one-way flow of information. Talking at or to someone does not imply successful communication. This only occurs when the receiver actually receives the message the sender intended to send. Message rejection, misinterpretation and misunderstanding are the opposite of effective communication.

The television advertising business is a science based on suspect data. This data is based upon a small sample, which decides how many households watch an actual programme, and doesn't even measure the commercial break.

Interactive communication exists to communicate clearly an advertising message, using existing media, to an open, focused and receptive mind based upon the principle it is not what you say, but how your consumer interacts with what you say which primarily determines how successfully the message gets across.

The changes in consumer perception and purchase behaviour produced by this form of communication are traditionally associated only with extensive advertising campaigns involving high levels of frequency and the inherent inefficiencies that result from such efforts.

Now the long silence, the industrial interruption of the human conversation, is coming to an end.

Not all the blame for bland, formulaic advertising, however, lies with the advertising industry. Many clients are also to blame. Chief marketing officers, with an average tenure of less than three years, have become loath to take risks.

In their drive to meet growth targets and cost-accountability, they rely heavily on research techniques, such as testing ads in front of focus groups, leading, inevitably, to least-common-denominator ads.

And that is the awful truth about marketing and advertising. It broadcasts messages to people who simply don't want to listen or see them.

Every advertisement, press release, publicity stunt and give-away designed by the marketing department, or advertising agency is coloured by the fact all their hard work and planning is being presented to a public which doesn't ask to hear or see it.

Let's look back at what I discussed regarding the number of actual 30-second spot ads viewed per week by the average American. You'll recall each individual sees about 120 television advertisements a week. The networks average about 4,000 commercials a week.

I also emphasise to you the Royal Mail in the UK commissioned research which produced a similar picture, again decribed earlier.

It is clear from the likes of the above that television advertising is not seen by many of the audience out there.

Just one of the examples why marketing departments should fire their advertising agency immediately and commence using interactive communication, it is so much more effective.

And stay far, far away from the Oscars at 1.7million (ish) a pop.

The future of advertising

During all our research, one constant shone through. Marketing is conversations.

Current conventional mass media is a weak conductor of knowledge and comprehension. This is because of a number of factors, however the main reason is, they are non-interactive communication vehicles, in other words 'conversations' cannot take place.

Research shows interaction raises a communication's learning effectiveness.

The one problem facing interactive advertising is the fact it has become a cliché in recent years, without any very clear or consistent definition of what the word means or how it is supposed to work.

Properly executed, it has none of the woolly theorising which lies behind the arguments about various forms of so-called interactive communication using direct marketing and electronic media (most of which involves, at best, the minimum of true interactivity).

It is practical, down-to-earth, and uses a readily comprehensible and verified mechanism to expand the relevance and salience of advertising and other forms of marketing communication. It can be applied to all major media and to various other forms of communication, including new media. There is no theoretical reason why it should not also be applied to packaging designs or product literature.

The basic elements of interactive communication are very simple, as all communication should be. The target audience, or any part of them, are provided with a game, comprising of a quiz together with multiple choice answers.

This takes the reader/viewer through the detail of a commercial or advertisement and focuses their interest and attention on the product's selling points. The questionnaire is (usually) presented as an exercise in getting the public's opinions about the products. The effect is to combine the techniques of programmed learning and game playing to fix the advertising message in consumers' minds.

The programme is very flexible and can be distributed by mail, door-to-door, as a handout in shopping malls, or as a newspaper or magazine insert.

The traditional, though now out-dated, model of communication against which advertising has been judged is a one-way process whereby a sender sends a message to a receiver, who is then expected to absorb and act upon it. Although any consumer-aware advertising person knows well that consumers use ads, rather than the reverse, the practice in most agencies remains the traditional one of pushing ads out towards the market and hoping for a response.

In the face of growing clutter of advertising messages and the increasing ability of consumers to screen out unwanted commercials and ads, there is also a growing problem for advertisers in breaking through the surrounding noise.

By presenting advertisements in the form of a game, it alters the consumer's perception to the content, making the communication process far more effective, by providing an enjoyable mechanism for consumers to become involved with the brand and its advertising message.

This meets the desire, evident among consumers, to open up a dialogue with at least some of the manufacturers or service companies whose products they buy. It feeds consumers' evident wish to be better informed about what it is they are being asked to buy.

By getting consumers to make a commitment to finding out more about an advertiser's offer, the interactive technique can create the conditions for positive attitudes towards the advertiser and positive learning about the product advertised.

In addition to providing this encouragement for consumers to focus on the brand and to develop for themselves the steps of the argument which should lead to a purchase, the technique can provide the advertiser with valuable feedback about both the product and its advertising. This is a dialogue which can benefit both sides, and be seen to be doing so.

By its very nature, the technique is totally accountable, so much so it is, as far as I can tell, the most heavily researched concept in the history of marketing communication.

Many of the world's largest independent research companies have measured the incremental increases just one exposure to an interactive programme can bring, what follows is a very brief summary as the effectiveness of the technique over all other forms of commercial communication:

Interactive multi-brand print "events" in Great Britain, Australia, Japan, USA, average results:

Four (4) weeks post

	% Did not see "Event"	% Saw "Event"	% Change Plus/Minus.
Aided brand awareness	68%	81%	+19
Past four (4) week purchase	11%	18%	+70
Next four (4) weeks purchase	9%	15%	+76
Comprehension of key Selling messages	49%	65%	+32
Persuasive power of key selling messages	22%	30%	+37

Representing results from a wide variety of product categories including:
Kellogg's Cornflakes; Carter Wallace beauty products; Cheseborough Ponds Skin Care; Revlon; Silkience; Weight Watchers; Commodore Computers; Nissan Automobiles; Toyota.

Research Source: AGB; BMR; Gallup; MRCA; NOP.

Marketing faces a tectonic shift

This has been signalled in the writings of such people as Regis McKenna in 1999, with his take on relationship marketing, and Don Pepper and Martha Rodgers, in 1997, with their one-to-one marketing gospel. This shift is also apparent in books reporting on the consumer psyche such as *The Experience Economy* by Joe Pine and Jim Gilmore, as well as in *The Dream Society* by Rolf Jensen. This shift is seen in the emergence of one of the biggest buzz terms in marketing today, customer relationship management and in the rapid rise of specialised technology behind another big buzz word, personalisation.

Unlike previous major developments in marketing, this shift is not driven by the cognoscenti of marketing, but by the confluence of two culture-shaping events, the internet and a matured (in years) consumer population. The latter event is changing the fundamental ethos of society.

The wrenching forces reshaping marketing are changing its foundations from a primarily objective base to a primarily subjective base. If it's not very clear what we mean, just think of traditional marketing as an objective marketing model which is numbers-based (statistics, probability theory, etc) and think of a subjective marketing model as behaviour-based, especially behaviour at the level of the individual. Subjective models are ideal for all the various forms of relationship marketing.

Abraham Maslow, the famous psychologist and creator of Maslow's heirarchy of needs, is quoted as saying: "If the only tool a man has is a hammer, then everything looks like a nail to him." If not the only tool, the primary tool in marketing has been mathamatics, so every consumer looks like a number through the lens of objective marketing models. Sure, by the time research results get to drawing boards, numbers start looking like real people, sort of. But, usually, hardly anyone relates to these cardboard personalities as real, and this detracts from message effectiveness.

People develop strong bonds when empathetic connections exist between parties involved in a relationship. The term customer loyalty has become a mantra, but we've never read any words about the criticality of empathetic linkage in fostering customer loyalty.

That's because most marketing is still based on objective models which play down the importance of behaviour. Objective marketing is more conducive to mental manipulation of consumers, than to establishing empathic linkages.

Many marketing directors have told us all, time and time again, in so many words: "At the end of the day, marketing is a numbers game. To increase sales, you increase exposure to get an increase in the number of consumers in your traffic flow." But protagonists of the various relationship marketing philosophies say things have changed. Customers are defining marketing. That moves the discipline from its objective, numbers-defined foundations to a subjective feelings-defined foundation that Pine and Gilmore call "the experience economy," and Jensen calls "The Dream

Society."

Marketers have been trying to meet the challenges of the experience economy mainly with technology. Personalisation software, such as those offered by Net Perceptions and BroadVision, and multitudinous products sold as customer relationship management (CRM) tools are all about deployment of massive database systems to capture as many details about consumers as possible to gain maximum advantage over their minds. This is the prime intent of objective marketing models: conquest and control. Otherwise, what accounts for all the military metaphors used in marketing?

Authors Jensen, Pine and Gilmore implicitly tell us if consumers are not totally "unaffected by the external world", more of them than ever before project a strong bias against marketers' definitions of product worthiness in favour of their own independent evaluations. This is driving marketers toward the unfamiliar practice of adapting to consumers, as opposed to trying to conquer, control and change them. In the more autonomy-minded consumer universe now facing marketers, the power and control orientation of objective marketing models is being replaced with an ethos of collaboration with consumers.

Getting in sync with this massive transformation of marketing is not easy, bearing in mind that we've been constrained by the equivalent of Maslow's hammer on math dominated, control-minded, objective marketing models.

Tom Stoppard's play *Arcadia*, best sums up the current situation: "A door like this has been opened five or six times since we got up on our hind legs. It's the best possible time to be alive when almost everything you thought you knew was wrong."

However well it worked in the past, and Proctor & Gamble offers vivid testimony to the fact it did, the objective marketing model is mostly wrong now.

Our minds are conditioned by the past, not the future. So we want to keep doing things the way we always have done them, even when results become ever more disappointing. But, every now and then, the ground beneath us shifts so dramatically as to make much of what we thought we knew so wrong it becomes clear we have to forge new beliefs or fail. These are such times in marketing. In today's more subjective-minded marketplace, the behavioural proclivities of consumers as individuals must be the determining factor, not exotic maths, even though it will obviously continue to be a critical tool, but not the main tool.

Sergio Zyman, former Chief Marketing Officer, the Coca-Cola Company, also had this to say in his book:

"Simply put, the problem with marketing today is that for the past 20 or 30 years, marketers have become increasingly caught up with the trappings of marketing. They have been wowed by the glitz, the awards presentations, and the jetting off to do a 'shoot' on some tropical isle, and they have forgotten that their job is to sell stuff. As a result they haven't done a very good job of selling stuff, and they have tried to hide their failure to deliver results in a black box labelled 'Marketing is Magic.'

"Today, at most companies, marketing is ineffective and, therefore, considered to be strictly a nonessential activity. Many marketers and their bosses might not admit it, but just look at their actions. Whenever budgets are tight, marketing is one of the first things that gets cut."

The successor to the brand image will be the 'brand experience' which goes far beyond the attributes of a product, and thus, 'creativity' is no longer the final arbiter as to the success, or otherwise, of a marketing campaign.

It is, and will continue to be, the development of an interactive relationship which will cement the ongoing bonds between the seller and buyer, now and for the future.

It has now become critical to redefine the role of media and the message, to develop an understanding of the behavioural dynamics of perception and interaction which were neglected during the explosive growth of advertising in the 1970s and '80s.

We have to accept the days of traditional advertising are over, where advertising was a one-way process from the advertiser to the consumer and never the other way round; it was a statement from one to many. Now this whole one-way process will be reversed. Consumers will 'talk' to the client to access each advertiser as a product information source.

Make the networks accountable

From all I have read and experienced over the past decade, a consensus has formed among researchers that the power of television commercials to affect sales ranges from the insignificant to the non-existent.

I feel it is fair to say some of the most acclaimed and memorable ads of all time have been pretty awful at doing what they were created for i.e. sell products.

However, this is not the fault of the television stations, and it is unfair they should now be the subject of such soul searching.

The commercials sometime look good and yes, viewers have sometimes been known to enjoy them, but make them buy the product?

Again, this consensus is not the fault of the television industry.

When interactive "events" which I described earlier, have been prepared together with a direct request for the viewer to pay particular attention to participating television commercials, there has always been a substantial and measurable lift in brand awareness, message comprehension, which has always lead through to increases in sales.

To demonstrate the effectiveness of interactive programmes linked to terrestrial television here are just some examples of the increases recorded by independent research.

Increases in television advertising awareness as result of exposure to an interactive "Event":

Birds Eye Fish Fingers	+11 percent
Sunsilk Shampoo	+233 percent
Duracell Batteries	+200 percent
Plumrose (Canned) Ham	+400 percent
Sara Lee	+83 percent
Sources: AGB, NOP, Gallup	

These results are just the tip of the iceberg in demonstrating that terrestrial television aligned with interactive events can produce staggering increases in all key measurements including sales.

Despite all this evidence to the contrary, remember what Kate Bruges, the Marketing Director of J Walter Thompson, said to the American Advertising Association in 2003: "The conventional stuff won't ever go away".

And remember she added: "An awful lot of this unconventional stuff is the icing on the cake, that extra bit of media mileage. But it's never going to give you the cost-efficient mileage or get the message across consistently enough to a large enough number of people."

Well, there are many clients who are at least making some attempt to disengage from what has been fed to them for all these years and with good reason.

The first rule of advertising, obviously, is to get noticed but this is easier said than done. In the advertising arena everyone is trying to get noticed and this results in clutter. When every adult person is bombarded with millions of advertising messages a year, yes millions, to acknowledge and act upon even a small proportion of these messages is a huge call on our time.

And time is the one irreplaceable commodity more and more of us are guarding jealously.

However, marry terrestrial television to interactive 'events' and all these old problems fade away, because terrestrial television, together with interactive 'events', fundamentally alters the customer's perception of the commercial break. No longer is it regarded as an interruption, the advertising becomes a meaningful source of information.

Terrestrial television can still be highly effective, maybe more so than ever, if done right.

Say it often enough

Say what? "Advertising works."

The biggest exageration in the history of business, it makes Enron and its 'creative' practices all pale into insignificance.

In 1998 the respected advertising journal in the USA, *Advertising Age*, called in two professors of marketing from the Wharton School of Business.

The brief, within a reasonable budget: would they go away and conclusively prove advertising works. They would have a time frame of roughly six months to work within.

"Piece of cake" is what I understand they said.

At the end of six months they returned to the offices of *Advertising Age* and were reluctantly forced to admit: "There was not one shred of evidence available to establish advertising exclusively increased sales." However this was not the end of it, they also had to admit their research efforts indicated: "The effect of advertising appeared to be in the opposite direction." Both these quotes are from *Advertising Age* in 1998 about the effectiveness of advertising.

This was not the first time I had heard this. An article in The Times in 1984 reported the Newspaper Society had produced a study on the viewing of the commercial channels, it conducted this research by building in miniature television cameras into the set and filming what the audience did when the commercial break was shown. The results replicated the UK study from the 1970s mentioned previously, but figures showed five percent of the audience used the commercial break as an opportunity to make love. Someone showed some sense.

Despite all this evidence, and a multitude of other research studies, the advertising agencies totally ignored all this research , they did not recommend their clients spend their marketing pounds on more cost efficient media.

Instead, in my experience, they downgraded the results (if they acknowledged the research at all) and reverted to the mysterious mantras they always used on their clients.

One of the consistent examples used to justify this expenditure was how successful Saatchi & Saatchi had been in getting the Conservative government elected in 1979, and, if it can work for politicians, it must therefore work for toothpaste, or whatever.

As we have said elsewhere in this book, no advertising campaign has ever elected a government or politician, however because of the media hype the story has been told often enough to be believed.

When I presented my interactive programmes to another well-respected ad firm, to their account planner, account director and sundry other minions. After showing them all the evidence of interactive communication, when properly executed, works more effectively than advertising, they responded by saying: "We agree with everything you have said, and we can see the need for other clients and agencies to use your technique. However, by the time *our* commercials come to air they have been developed by our account planners so rigorously that they get seen on television."

That's just one example of how an agency ignores the obvious and can create totally meaningless statements so as to avoid not going on television.

I remember presenting the research results on a certain product within the yellow fat category, in Australia, to the manufacturers' advertising agency.

We had increased claimed purchase (DWB) by four percent, excellent in the difficult market being experienced at the time.

I reasoned with the account director for an hour as to why they should retain the category and to repeat in the latest programme.

I was getting nowhere, just then, her phone rang.

"Yes," she said, "oh no, I'll be right up." She turned to me, "Paul, I'm sorry, but I have just heard from the creative director. The 30-second commercial we shot in Bermuda recently has not come out well. I have to go and review the rushes and then arrange to re-shoot in Surfers Paradise up in Queensland."

Only goes to prove they could have saved the client heaps of money if they had gone to Queensland in the first place.

So, the poor old client probably ended up paying for extra footage, yet still the agency didn't want to talk about a four percent increase in sales.

Hooray for advertising. Agency people get to travel, first class, at the client's expense.

Clients have also been known to enjoy these perks. On another occasion I was presenting the research on the results of a product using the technique to the brand manager at their office in the UK.

Our interactive programme had produced a sales increase of three percent, a huge increase in that particular segment of the market, the detergent market.

Again, I reasoned for an hour with this particular brand manager as to why he should retain the category and participate in the next interactive programme.

Weariness overcame him, at the end of the hour his only reason for not proceeding was: "Paul, I like to go home turn on the television and say to my wife, there is my product on television."

And therein lies the rub, even the brands are not necessarily going on to television to increase sales. They like to go onto television for the prestige of being on television. They like to go on 'shoots', and all the other perceived 'glittery' reasons associated with television.

Of course, one of the other reasons they find it difficult to make a decision is the fact no other advertising agency has ever produced accountability, results stemming from their huge expenditures on commercial television, so there is little to make reasoned judgements against. So they dismiss interactive programmes for things like, "being not sexy". Yes, as indicated before, I heard that one too.

To return to a favourite theme of mine, mentioned above, of advertising campaigns getting governments elected, in my opinion, it doesn't. And never has. The Conservative government was elected in 1979 not for anything produced by Saatchi & Saatchi, but by the overwhelming public discontent with the Labour government. They had had enough of a government which had failed dismally to deliver economic competence. Similarly, the New Labour government came to power in 1997, not because of some advertising gimmick, but because people were still smarting from the economic humiliation of Black Wednesday in September 1992.

To suggest some slick little advertising slogan was a far stronger reason for changing a government than what had gone on in reality is an insult to the intelligence of the average British voter. This is one of the problems with advertising,. They, the practitioners, really believe their slick, glittery 30-second television commercials really have the power to change peoples behaviour. When the reality is they don't and can't.

Sleeping with the enemy

The worst of them all is the ex-advertising agency man, or woman, who leaves his agency to join a client to, very often, head up their marketing communication division as the new dynamic force, the guru, the gifted communicator.

On visiting one of these clients, we were met by his ex-advertising man who had the grandiose title of Advertising Director. The presentation had hardly started when he interrupted: "Don't start telling me television advertising doesn't work. I have evidence to the contrary."

When politely challenged, he had no evidence because there is none.

So, on what basis was he able to make this statement? Why, from his own experience of course. He had worked for so long in a large advertising group prior to attaining his current exulted status as Advertising Director, he now believed his own propaganda.

And this is why this chapter is titled, Sleeping with the enemy. Because dear client, this is what you are doing. Your new appointment, let me repeat, is unlikely to know anything significant about the process of communication. He will, undoubtedly, still believe the old mantras advertising agencies spout forth, including the biggest of them all, "advertising produces sales".

Please don't think for one moment my tirade starts and finishes with advertising agencies, there are equally guilty parties elsewhere. The direct marketing agencies are becoming as pedantic as their 'above the line' counterparts, whereby some seem to exist to boast about their 'creativity'.

In fact, direct marketing has a wonderful opportunity to demonstrate to the major fast moving consomer goods (fmcg) companies their products could be more successful by going the direct interactive way.

In the spring of 1994, H J Heinz, the century-old, $7billion processed foods marketer, announced a massive shift in marketing priorities. The packaged goods marketer was going to eliminate entirely its $8million television budget for its famous '57' varieties of beans, ketchup, pickles, soups etc.

Instead, Heinz would use the brand-building money for direct mail. It was a great turnabout, switching all those monies from so-called 'above-the-line' expenditure (impressions), to 'below-the-line' (accountability).

Let me stress here, the management at Heinz was completely correct in its thinking, however it was sleeping with the enemy. It duly hired a direct marketing agency to execute the programme. The result? It was not a success. In my opinion, this was because not enough attention was paid to the one essential word in all of marketing - communication. The sad thing is, a wonderful opportunity to move away from advertising-as-usual was lost. A huge collective sign of relief could be heard all over London as the 'above-the-line' agencies crowed over the return to the old ways H J Heinz eventually had to conduct.

In a corporate statement, spotted in *Campaign and Marketing Week*, Heinz management said: "The proliferation of media channels and the associated fragmentation of consumer audiences has called into question the effectiveness of advertising for individual brands. Many marketers are asking themselves: Is there a better way of communicating individual brand messages to key consumers?"

We maintain there is a better way and this way is by adopting the true principles of marketing communication in an environment which is not getting any easier. Competition from retailer own-label and cheaper brands, including retailer value brands, continues to intensify. Large retailers are gaining information about individual customers through their frequent-buyer clubs and are using this information to direct own-label brands into the hands of known buyers of the manufacturers' products. The result? Own-label brands accounted for about 33 percent of supermarket sales of processed foods in the UK in 2006.

Above-the-line advertising clearly is not working to halt this decline in branded goods sales.

According to *Marketing Week*, *Campaign* and *Media Week*, the great multinational Unilever also had the courage to enter this form of marketing with their Jigsaw consortium, along with Kimberley Clark, Cadbury and originally, Bass. Yet another huge sign of relief could be heard, when the consortium announced the cessation of the programme.

If they got the communication right and affected consumer behaviour in the way they wanted, these companies could now have halved their colossal marketing budgets and, at the same time, would have improved the marketing of their products, by listening to their customers, telling the customers they were listening, acting upon their customers' demands and making these customers an integral part of the communication process.

One of the worst examples of sleeping with the enemy, is within the media itself. Advertising is the principal source of revenue for most of the commercial mass media throughout the world. In more and more instances, it is now the advertiser client who is paying.

The media no longer serves primarily as news and information producers. Rather it has become transmitters of commercial messages. Newspapers have to face up to the truth and stop fooling themselves they are in the 'newspaper business' and admit that they are primarily in the business of carrying advertising messages.

The relationship between advertising and the media, be it print, television or radio, has long been an incestuous one.

And, like all unhealthy relationships, there is no such thing as a free lunch, or in this case, television commercial.

Until recently, the belief in 'free television' was almost an article of faith. Yes, it has dramatically changed with the advent of satellite and cable offerings. But, commercial television never was 'free' to the consumer no matter what they may have thought in the past. Viewers didn't pay anything for it you, might say. But like many a stealth tax, it is paid in an indirect way, as part of the added cost of the products advertised. After all, someone had to pay and it proliferates today.

A paper published by J Walter Thompson, and reported in The Times in

2002, made no effort to hide the issue:

"There was a time, in ITV's early days, when one of the major programme companies took to announcing themselves as 'your free television service'. The Independent Television Authority (as the IBA then was) asked them to stop it, on the grounds that it is not true."

In America, advertising on television is known, fairly openly, as a 'brand tax', where advertising is seen as a built-in cost. A cost, which is automatically passed onto the consumer.

The advantage of commercial television then is, not that it is free, but that it appears to be free. It might be described, in terms of commercial television, as the enemy within your living room.

What they don't teach working in an advertising agency

The human desire for interaction.

If this had been taught, and the lesson put into everyday practise, then billions of pounds and dollars would never have been poured down the black hole of television advertising.

So, let's review the desire in terms of the marketing of products and, at the same time, hope those people working in, or, with advertising agencies read this simple lesson and learn a little of what they should have already known and been doing on behalf of their clients and in turn, their customers.

All advertising is a form of learning, whereby the advertiser is asking people to change their behaviour after learning the benefits of the products or services on offer. However, we all tend to filter out information which we do not want to hear. This clearly alters the effectiveness of conventional advertising in quite a dramatic way.

The final purchase decision is invariably a compromise and this leads to a certain amount of anxiety; the worry perhaps the decision was not the best or the right one. In order to minimise this anxiety the purchaser seeks to reinforce their choice and begins to take more notice of their chosen product's marketing communications.

Due to a lack of understanding of the communication process we have created a media society during the past 40 or 50 years, where the whole process has been de-humanised. There is now an extraordinary reduction in interaction because conventional advertising and marketing have become a one-way practice whereby information is disseminated in a passive form.

But people still have this desire to be taken account of. To affect change, to learn and personalise their relationship with their environment. There are a phenomenal number of reasons causing people to interact, going far beyond just giving them things.

When people agree to participate in truly interactive marketing programmes they are told their efforts and feedback are of positive help to the advertisers. And most important to the advertisers, by participating and becoming involved, they then learn and understand the advertising message, doing so at their own pace and to fit in with their schedule. Consequently, because they are being involved in the process of developing the product or service, it starts to re-personalise their relationship with the advertiser and their products.

This takes the consumer through the barrier of not wanting to address change and takes this compromise, the anxiety and worry perhaps the decision was not the best or the right one, out of the equation. In other words, there is no reason why they should not change from their usual brand in favour of this alternative that they have now learned, fulfils their needs better. Isn't this the ultimate market the advertiser is after, the people who use his competitors' products? Now the consumer can say: "Yes, I will change my behaviour and I have a very good reason, or series of reasons, why." They can adopt this position because they have a well informed opinion or have developed an image of why that product is appropriate for their needs.

Now the long silence, the industrial interruption of the human conversation is coming to an end.

With interactive communication, every product you can think of, from fashion to office supplies, can be discussed, and argued over. Rather like the olden days when one went to the open air market to do just that.

With one important exception, the manufacturer can now become involved with this give and take to everyone's advantage.

People want to talk about value. But, the value of a product and the company which sells them. Not just the price of something. Reputation, position and every other quality which can be subject to an opinion.

It has always been this way. The most effective form of advertising that there has ever been is word of mouth, which is of course, nothing more than a conversation. But, as we have examined, conventional advertising and marketing give little or no opportunity for the 'audience' to engage in any kind of conversation about the product or the company.

No opportunity to discuss value, reputation, position. It simply sends out a message of sorts, albeit a nice looking one with sublime attention to production values which in turn reflect the values of the brand. But, if it isn't telling the audience the information they desire and seek to make a decision or reinforce a decision already made, then just who is listening and, who is it for?

More dangerous for advertising-as-usual, is that one-way advertising doesn't enable customers to learn the truth behind product claims.

If true marketing is a conversation and there's no allowance made for a return message, a feedback from the customer, then what does advertising-as-usual actually do?

We hold the strong view advertising-as-usual in any form and for any subject, is pitiable. It's not funny. It most certainly is not interesting and it doesn't even know who we, the customers, are or seemingly care for that matter. All advertising-as-usual wants us to do is buy.

Without a doubt, television is the best medium ever created for advertising-as-usual. The trouble is it doesn't actually seem to sell a great deal of product.

Why?

Consider this, you might well think marketing departments and their advertising agencies talk about communication and sales. Put simply, they don't.

As I have discussed, within an advertising agency scant attention, if any, is paid to the actual process of communication and as for an interest in sales, well that's a joke, to put it bluntly.

They are concerned with crafting messages. But not to sell products, If they did, surely they would be happy enough to be paid upon results. Actual changes in behaviour and actual sales increases resulting from the advertising they have created. Are we alone in never having come across any agency willing to adopt this stance? The creative director loves to produce television commercials smart enough to include on their show reel. And who knows, like some of his predecessors maybe they might get to direct a movie. The account director? All he wants to do is keep the client happy. Nobody, it seems, is really concerned with the actual job of selling a product, apart from, of course, the client. Sadly, however, they in turn are fed the belief that creativity is king. They get sucked in to advertising-as-usual, because after all, doesn't the agency know best? Isn't that what he is paying them for? And don't they have years of experience and expertise? Well, yes they do, but expertise in, yes, you're getting there, advertising-as-usual.

So, they happily carry on the usual treadmill of crafting messages.

In the form of advertisements; press releases; TV commercials and many other forms of what they genuinely believe is 'communication'.

Marketing departments, through their handmaiden advertising agencies paint a happy picture. But, no one out there in the real world of family life, believes what they are delivering and trying to force on them. The reality is, we all know better and have been taught by a lifetime of experience to turn down the volume when confronted with a television commercial explaining a product is the best and brightest available or failing that, even walk out of the room and do something else.

The old way of advertising, pouring out vast amounts of information in the desperate hope somebody somewhere will connect certainly had one effect, it depersonalised and dehumanised the whole process of communication.

Thus wasting even more millions of client money.

Consider their model of reach and frequency, who does this really serve? Does it serve the consumer, or does it provide the revenue the advertiser seeks?

It was so easy, in fact, that each adult person in this country, according to a client we were discussing this with, receives thousands of advertising messages each week. In the advertising and marketing world, we call it commercial clutter. More appropriately, it should be called 'meaningless noise'.

Just consider the ways in which your customer can enter into a dialogue with you? You may have an 0800 number, which would be a good start if they could speak to a real person. But, in these days of automation and with luck, eventually getting through to a call centre, unless you tire with frustration or collapse with fatigue, where is the dialogue there? Hey, they could go to the trouble of writing to you. But they are making the effort of putting pen to paper or more likely, tapping the keyboard these days, having found the customer care email address online. And finally, they sit and hope it does indeed reach the right person and their message is responded to. Sadly, it is often the case the process takes so long that they have lost interest, but more importantly lost faith, in your company and your product. Everyone in marketing is fully aware it costs more to find a customer than it does to keep one. But, so far, there has not been much opportunity for this customer to easily talk to you.

One of the problems advertising has created is the process of dehumanising people. Advertising apparently, forgets every customer and every prospective customer is a human being with a constantly evolving set of attitudes and opinions. And if advertising is aware, then it does very little to cater for this all important human factor.

The other problem is advertising agencies don't realise customers don't really like advertisements.

An advertising agency had the following statement on the form for their creative brief: "The audience doesn't like you, doesn't trust you, and they can get rid of you immediately. Now go and create some advertising."

This precisely sums up the essence of today's adversarial relationship between the customer and advertising people. They really don't like each other, customers tolerate advertisements, but they don't really like them in terms of the content.

However, when you create a dialogue out of your advertising, it turns passive information into active, meaningful advertising and actually alters behaviour during the learning process. It cuts through the psychological barriers, which prevent the individual from changing their attitude and behaviour towards brands.

Interactive communication, in whatever form, reflects a shift from monologue to dialogue, in dealing with customers. The results are a reversal of traditional consumer and producer roles, with the consumer dictating exactly how he or she would like to be served. New customers expect to asked about their individual preferences and treated, to the most extreme degree possible, as if these preferences are being respected. This is, and should be now, the future of advertising, and television commercials, the mainstay of advertising agencies, will hardly be immune from these forces of change. The then Chairman and CEO of Procter & Gamble, Ed Artzt, shocked the advertising community when he addressed the American Association of Advertising Agencies: "From where we stand today, we can't be sure that ad-supported television programming will have a future in the world being created, a world of video-on-demand, pay-per-view, and subscription television. Within the next few years, surely before the end of the decade, consumers will be choosing among hundreds of shows and pay-per-view movies. They'll have dozens of home shopping channels. They'll play hours of interactive video games. And for many of these, maybe most, no advertising at all. If that happens, if advertising is no longer needed to pay most of the cost of home entertainment, then advertisers like us will have a hard time achieving the reach and frequency we need to support our brands."

A chilling thought. That speech was made in 1994.

Agencies virtually ignored everything except television

The current model of advertising was invented in the 1960s when product choice was much more limited and people were easier to stereotype into categories like income, gender and class. It was much easier for advertisers to target people and bombard them with sales messages.

Today's marketplace is different and all the old certainties are gone. To be effective in your communication, it is sound advice to start with the premise you know nothing about the people you believe your product is aimed at.

Advertising has become too parochial, too introspective, too convinced by its own hyperbole.

Two or three thousand, what would be described as, creative people, dominate advertising.

However, a major change is afoot and advertising, long regarded as the ultimate weapon in marketing, particularly the once mighty television commercial, is now seen as complacent and increasingly ineffective.

Consequently, the power of the creative is diminishing. And why is this a good thing for clients and their customers? Because in my view, very often, these creatives have been the barrier holding back progress.

It is amazing ,when you consider the many excellent marketing ideas which have been available. However, the promoters of such ideas eventually gave up selling to advertising agencies because all advertising agencies wanted was to get their clients onto television.

That it might not be the ideal medium was totally ignored.

My experience was typical; I developed the most potent, effective and accountable marketing communication programme – ever.

When I started in the business, I was introduced to the futurologist Alvin Toffler who, when hearing of what I was doing simply said: "Persevere, but remember vested interests will be against you."

Was he ever right.

I was confident what I was proposing would be more effective and I would be giving clients the very communication programme they needed. So confident I and some partners borrowed $3.5million from venture capitalists.

The pitch to clients was beguiling and had never been heard before: "You pay nothing to come into the programme. However, you agree to accept the findings of a stringent purchase study, to be conducted by the independent Market Research Corporation of America (MRCA).

"Based on those findings would you then pay us a 15 per cent commission on the incremental increases in sales produced."

The clients fell about laughing, they had never had such an offer from any of their advertising agencies. "Where do we sign?"

We mail delivered 19 million copies of *Shopper's Voice*. Because it was mail delivered we could have Test and Control cells as next door neighbours, thus allowing us to measure changes in behaviour and actual purchase amongst those who had received the programme, Test, and those who had not, Control.

Obviously, Control was exposed to everything else the featured brands were involved in. MRCA are on record as saying: "It was the (then) most precise purchase study ever carried out by us."

To get a perspective, no advertising campaign had ever had such a high degree of accountability put behind it after just one exposure.

To cut a long story short, when we presented the increase in sales figures to Colgate Palmolive, we said the results indicated a fee of $780,000 based upon the agreed MRCA formulae. All Colgate could say to us as they handed us the cheque, "Could we redefine the rules of this game please?"

The figure arrived at was due to the results gained from a double page interactive spread inside our Shopper's Voice magazine. But, interactive in our terms is where the communication process became two-way not based upon any electronic gizmo. The recipients were, for the first time in any advertising context, given the opportunity to be involved with the brands and be part of the communication process.

Colgate had never experienced such a result from all their billions of dollars invested in conventional advertising and they directed us to their advertising agency.

In hindsight, it is amusing to recall the many, many excuses the agency made not to use us and they stifled the idea. And in those days if the agency said no, very often the client accepted their judgement.

When presented with a way of making their contribution totally accountable, why did they bring down the portcullis? Well, you can draw your own conclusions.

Don't rush into change too fast

Currently, advertising agencies are still dancing on the head of a pin called a 30-second television commercial. The really terrifying aspect of all this is that advertising agencies have come up with no new ideas as to how to combat clutter; or even customer mistrust and outright avoidance of traditional advertising. And it is the media which is suffering as a result of such communication incompetence, especially terrestrial television.

And yet, these ideas have always been around, however what satisfied the creative ego was the creative director and his acolytes swanning around with the hottest Hollywood movie producer.

As I have mentioned before, the attitude within advertising agencies still is: "The answer is a television commercial, what's your question?"

Alone the 30-second television ad is not the right answer. But, if you add the right supporting communication process, the existing media can be much more effective and accountable.

In the past, advertisers used to load the television production cost by hiring an outlandishly expensive Hollywood movie director. It satisfied all the egos involved, but, and here is the really weird thing, the consumer couldn't care less about who directs the commercial, all they wanted was the right information that would allow them to like and buy the product/service

We must use ways which make existing media much more effective. They do exist but have been totally ignored by advertising agencies.

In the advertising industry's days of dominance, peopled believed it could change the ways consumers thought and behaved, not just influence them to favour one brand in a category they were already considering.

In earlier days there was a faith, when there was little objective difference among products, an emotion-laden image is always used as a motivator.

Much of this sense of advertising's enormous power, and the almost inevitable effectiveness of image advertising, grew as mass advertising followed mass manufacturing in the 1950s and '60s

Marketing people are moving away from that totally inaccurate picture. However, fmcg marketing people still haven't cottoned on to the fact you can sell more goods to less people, and still be more effective, if you understand the benefits of 'conversations' and interactive television.

Now, customised products are coming back. Modern manufacturing has attained the ability to replicate, in its own way, the Old World of choice.

Advertising agencies have lost sight of their primary goal: to sell the product. Fortunes are wasted on hip, award-winning commercials which I think often fail to even communicate the brand.

The reality of business demands advertising answers to the bottom line. Simply by adding interactive communication to your schedules you can reduce spend and make your existing advertising totally accountable.

Which will demonstrably affect your bottom line and, much to the (antici-pated) great disgust of advertising agencies, clients can substantially reduce their horrific marketing investment.

Terrestrial television can then breathe a sigh of relief and get on with what it is good at, producing good programming.

A new media age

A new media age appears to be dawning, one in which many of the old rules of salesmanship will no longer apply. It is hard to believe anyone will sit still for numbing repetitions of intrusive jingles, or for 30-second spots of unrewarding commercials.

I can recall a time when the various utilities used to keep a television set running in their control centres to enable them to adjust for the sudden surge of electricity and the increase in water consumption when the commercial break appeared.

In a world where people can talk back to their television sets, the age-old question of just how advertising works, and whether it works at all, may finally be answered.

Conventional mass media is a weak conductor of knowledge and comprehension. This is because it is non-interactive communication vehicle. Communication research shows interaction raises a communication's learning effectiveness. Advertisers must search for, and use, an innovative mass media which provides interactive communication. Otherwise, they have little chance to effectively generate quality awareness or communication learning in the target consumers.

Farewell to the passive television ad of old.

Viewers are becoming impatient with television's linear flow and are increasingly using the opportunities available to them to avoid the intentions of advertisers and programme makers.

Too much advertising is focused on a market place that is gone. Manufacturing has changed. Marketing has changed. Advertising has not, and it is no wonder that clients are losing faith in it.

This decline in confidence has been going on for several years. Much of this sense of advertising's enormous power and the almost inevitable effectiveness of image advertising grew as mass advertising followed mass manufacturing in the '50s and '60s. Mass manufacturing led to one-size-fits-all products. Local, individualised, and speciality products disappeared, and the mass consumerism was achieved via mass advertising.

Advertising has been clinging to a world which existed 10, 20, even 30 years ago as if it were trying not to notice it's vanished. Advertising has to modernise and change.

Marketing, by definition is 'dynamic' and 'ongoing', and yet agencies are working under the same old values.

Its effectiveness will regenerate itself because the information content of advertising is a fundamental necessity for the efficient conduct of a complex and free market place.

Instead of asking: "When are the good times coming back?" we should be applying ourselves to doing advertising in ways which are right for the time we live in.

At the same time consumers have changed, technology and the proliferation of media are transforming the science of marketing to them. Now, companies increasingly can aim their messages to carefully pinpointed consumers through direct mail.

Increasingly, when big companies see their business decline, they do not follow tradition and pour more money down the drain.

There is no denying that marketers want more accountability. Struggling to meet financial goals in markets which often grow no faster than the population as a whole, packaged goods companies have been riding hard on their brand managers to produce quarterly sales results. The impact of image-building advertising on sales can often be tough to see. Not so with price discounts or coupons, which give sales a quick, easily measured kick. People are saying: "I can't wait for advertising to work. I've got to turn these pounds around more quickly."

The challenge of the century. How to reach your target market.

In many ways television is an advertising, not communication, medium. As television declines in the face of competition from the new media, conventional advertising will decline with it.

"Advertising" is an outmoded concept since media advertising is just one of many ways of communicating with customers.

The ability to boost sales automatically via advertising and promotion, taken for granted in the 1980s, has become a lost art in the 21st century. In an era of shifting consumer values and lifestyles, a cluttered communications environment and an overflow of information, niche marketing will become increasingly important.

While technology and multiple messages are necessary elements in mass communication, they are far from sufficient for any actual communication to take place.

Mass communication, if it is to be successful, must take on many characteristics of interpersonal communication. Audience members must be able to give feedback. Media practitioners must be sensitive to the information contained in the feedback. The give and take can result in understanding or real communication.

Advertising agencies need to change their limited definition of communication and media and see themselves as specialist's in a range of techniques.

The decline of the golden age of advertising agencies centred on the creative television commercial has commenced. Unless they wake up to the changes that are occurring they risk becoming the first dinosaurs of the new media age.

Back to the future

I started working on this book around 2002, so felt I should end with a review of the changes which have taken place since the advent of new technology and the growth of the internet as an advertising medium.

So, what changes have taken place in commercial communication?

Simply put nothing. Advertising agencies are still wedded to the 30-second television commercial. The really terrifying aspect of all this is that advertising agencies have come up with no new ideas as to how to combat clutter; or even customer mistrust and outright avoidance of traditional advertising.

As I mentioned before, the attitude within advertising agencies still is: "The answer is a television commercial, what's your question?"

I find it amazing to note that junk mail is alive and growing.

Whoever said: "The more things change, the more they remain the same," was spot on when applying that maxim to the advertising world.

Clutter. The dreadful word came into vogue in the late 1960s and was applied to the proliferation of advertising messages the consumer could be exposed to during the course of his or her working day. More accurately the term was "commercial clutter", however as I have stated, I much prefer "meaningless noise".

Well the growth of digital television and radio, together with the proliferation of television channels means this "clutter" has become a downright deluge of information, of all sorts, and still the advertising world has no answer to the problem, and, frankly, they don't want it to end. To the advertising agencies, 'commercial clutter' means bigger profits, so stuff the client and lets get more messages out there.

We live in an over informed society and people everywhere are turning away from the commercial information spewed out from all media, it is of no interest or relevance to them at all.

Remember when the internet and online marketing were going to spell the end of the direct mail business? Well, it hasn't exactly worked out that way.

During 2005, United States marketers sent more than 114 billion pieces of direct mail. Catalogues, credit card solicitations, coupons and the like, an increase of roughly 15 percent from five years before, according to the United States Postal Service. And in the same year, for the first time, the volume of bulk mail, which is all direct mail, exceeded first class.

As the world becomes more digital, there is a need for tangible experiences. And there's nothing like a piece of paper.

From the consumer's point of view, there is some relief from this deluge of information, email from marketers can be blocked by spam filters, and reaching customers vie email often requires them to agree to be on a company's solicitation list. Direct mail, on the other hand, lands in mailboxes without an invitation, but does not seem to be considered as annoying by consumers, in part because it often is related to their past purchases.

Ad agencies are starting to change as well in response to the growth in direct mail.

Most companies did not even include spending on direct mail or promotions as an advertising expense, instead lumping them into general sales expenses and calling such spending "below the line".

It was anything not considered important enough for the board of directors or CEO to know about, because all they were ever talking about before at cocktail parties was television commercials.

Ad executives expect the boom in direct mail to continue.

However, among consumers, a major change was underway, which I would best sum up by stating: "We are immune to advertising. Just forget it."

That was a theme a few years ago as part of the *Cluetrain Manifesto*, true then, even truer to day.

Elvis said it best: "We can't go on together with suspicious minds."

Companies need to come down from their ivory towers and talk to the people with whom they hope to create relationships.

Public relations does not relate to the public. Companies are deeply afraid of their markets.

Up until a few years ago, advertising was the province of a privileged few to the passive many. Now, the ownership of moving images has passed into the hands of practically everybody and the articulation of moving images has passed into the hands of everybody with access to a phone, laptop or digital camera. We can now have our say.

In essence, the behaviour of the audience is moving from passive to active participation, so television watching or listening to radio in the future will be a very different and less sedentary experience than it has been in the past 80 years.

Ultimate power isn't with brand owners or even with broadcasters, and most certainly doesn't exist with the advertising agencies at all. It's with the viewer. And it's the on/off switch.

Given that the traditional interruption model of television advertising is no longer as effective as it was a decade ago, and coupled with the rise of personal video recorders (PVR) which permit viewers to record programmes free of advertising, broadcast sponsorship is potentially more attractive for brand owners than traditional advertising.

As a result, brand owners and their agencies have started to explore other hybrid-broadcast sponsorship models, such as product placement, advertiser-funded programming (AFP), as well as controlling their own television and radio channels.

However, be careful what you believe on the internet: there's a growing chance you're being hoaxed by a cynical PR firm, here comes yet another trend whichis far more pernicious.

A "flog" is a fake blog which purports to chronicle an ordinary consumer's passion for a business or a product, typically without the company behind it declaring an interest. It is a scandalously dishonest practice.

For example, take Laura and Jim, an ordinary couple who recently drove a camper van across America and stopped over for free each night at their nearest Wal-Mart car park. Their likeable amateurish travel journal, Wal-Marting across America, chronicled all the decent, hard working Wal-Mart employees they encountered during their stopovers, all of whom seemed to have great stories about the company.

Lo and behold, the couple turned out to be professionals paid by Wal-Mart's PR firm, Edelman, and folksy Jim was revealed to be a professional newspaper photographer. Laura used the blog to come clean, admitting she "should have done a better job" telling her story.

How widespread is the trend? It is hard to tell, as the floggers are hardly looking to admit to their duplicity. But there is an awful lot of fake amateurism out there, from the widely viewed YouTube clips by "lonelygirl15" exposed as a professional actress, to the marketing agencies who will pay ordinary bloggers to talk up clients' products in their everyday musings. One such agency, PayPerPost, claims it pays bloggers as much as hundreds of pounds each month simply for writing "their honest opinions" about sponsors' products. Their honest opinions, clearly, never compromised by that commercial relationship.

The advertising industry is having trouble figuring out whether these are the best of times or the worst of times.

They are the worst of times because the business model on which the industry was built, hefty profit margins for pitching mass products through mass media to mass markets, is finally collapsing around them.

None of this happened overnight. The process began more than 20 years ago. In the search for what went wrong, one path leads to industry consolidation.

Starting in the early 1980s, the independent agencies were bought up by big holding companies. The problem, of course, was the buyers paid ridiculously high prices for firms where the talent and the clients can walk out the door anytime. Some did, heading for nimbler, cheaper and more creative regional shops. So the consolidators figured they had no choice but to buy those, too. To that were added foreign firms, public relations firms, research firms and production agencies, on the theory they could provide one-stop shopping to their global corporate clients. When internet marketing firms became all the rage in the late 1990s, they overpaid for those too.

As it turned out, much of this consolidation was based on false premises.

There weren't really many economies of scale to be achieved by combining all these competing agencies. Not much co-operation ever developed among former rivals. Corporate clients still wanted to be pitched by agencies, not conglomerates, and were less interested in one-stop shopping than first thought. And in time realised to get breakthrough work, they had to look beyond their primary agency to upstart firms.

Things haven't exactly worked out as planned, including for investors, whose annual returns have ranged from mediocre to awful. Creative-services firms have proven ill suited to the demands of public shareholders and analysts, with their fixation on quarterly earnings targets and double-digit growth. The emphasis on cost cutting and meeting financial goals dampened the enthusiasm for risk-taking at the heart of creative advertising.

The mantra became figure out what the client wants, do it, get paid. Because agencies are generally paid on the basis of fixed retainers, hourly billing rates and media commissions, there is no financial difference between delivering a blockbuster ad and delivering a mediocre one.

Not all the blame for bland, formulaic advertising, however, lies with the advertising industry. Many clients are also to blame. Chief marketing officers, with an average tenure of less than three years, have become loath to take risks.

Because so much time and money is shifting to the internet, none of the old rules apply. Now, it is the clients who are pushing the agencies for change, and the agencies are finally examining how they are organised, how they are paid and how they conceive of their jobs. As a result, after a decade of fighting changes, the industry is coming around to embrace them. Changes once seen as frightening are now being viewed, at least at the top of the ad business, as opportunities.

The need for change is not governed by the development of superior technology, but by the failure of current advertising.

Advertising agencies have, for far too long, been using assumptions of the world past, where a 30-second television commercial was the answer to every marketing communication problem.

Conventional wisdom has long subscribed to the phrase "advertising works". The argument is Western economies have produced individual wealth, however, advertising has not adequately addressed consumers' needs, such as the human need for interaction, and, more importantly, accountability.

All the new technology does is to cause us to reconsider the values of one-way communication.

But, the problem for agencies, advertisers and media owners, is working out how, in a perfect market, they can tip the balance in their favour. It's a problem to which they have no real answer, except to try to get to grips with the New World order as best they can.

Unfortunately, the answer to this is an indication as to the problem existing within advertising agencies since time immemorial, which is the scant attention, if any at all, which is paid to the actual process of communication.

Together with the slavish devotion to creativity and media buying.

The days are numbered for television ads' dominance. However, surprisingly, many marketers remain reluctant to look at new media alternatives, in part because they don't know how to use them. They don't know what to replace television with.

Clients continue to spent a majority of money in a very dinosauristic medium perhaps they are hoping they can retire before change happens.

A new model is desperately required. The painful thing is the new model may be totally different and may be less profitable.

Most certainly the correct model of communication is totally different, it does not have a slavish adherence to the reach frequency model so beloved by the advertising industry, nor does it rely upon creativity. However, properly executed it is highly profitable and, finally, allows total accountability full rein.

The advertising industry is in great danger of becoming hypnotised by another new glossy media gimmick - digital.

Again, alas, no mention of the communication process.

Take a global view of the television, radio, telecom and wireless communications industries, which command aggregated annual revenues of £840billion (Source: WARC November '06).

Then apply the old maxim I mentioned before: "50 percent of my advertising is wasted but I don't know which 50 percent," and that gives you a world-wide wastage factor of £420billion. Here, please bear in mind I have heard an experienced ad manager at a multinational say his estimate of wastage was more like 85 percent, so it could very well be our figures are inaccurate.

To be more than fair to advertising we will discount the £420billion figure by halving it to £210 billion and then multiply it by the past 10 years and a shocking (yet conservative because we halved the figure) total of £2,100billion of advertising wastage materialises, as we said earlier, bigger than Enron

The "new model" has been around for years, it has been totally ignored by the advertising industry until now, when clutter and lack of attention to advertising have forced clients to reconsider their huge advertising investments.

As I said earlier, bigger than Enron.

I titled this book *Television Killed Advertising*, because there was more than a touch of truth in that. Up until the advent of television, advertising agencies played a bigger role in the preparation of the entire clients' advertising collateral.

They concerned themselves with packaging design, with the preparation of sales aids, they worked closely with the clients on the preparation of marketing plans and much more. It was the natural inclination of clients to automatically call their agency when any marketing problem arose.

Then came commercial television.

Almost overnight the agencies surrendered their traditional role of guardian of the brand image and rushed off in another direction. The production of lucrative television commercials, for they were ever so profitable.

Allowing specialist design firms, business consultants, accountants, etc, to take over the bulk of their still highly profitable business activities.

Hence *Television Killed Advertising*.

The other potential title, which has remained a theme throughout the book came to me when I was studying the annual advertising expenditure of the USA, UK, France, Germany, Spain, Japan, and Australia. I realised if you applied the statement, attributed to many people, about wasting 50 percent of advertising expenditure, then the costly ineffectiveness of advertising was huge. Then factor in the fact there has never been any true accountability, then the fact this wastefulness has been going on since the end of the Second World War. Then the truth is the scandal really is:

Bigger than Enron.

Acknowledgements

First of all a special thank you to Oxo cubes.

Not so long ago, I attended a very pleasant dinner party in Denier, southern Spain. Sitting to my right was a charming woman whose face was extremely familiar although I couldn't put a name to the face. When we started discussing what we did respectively, I discovered that I was sitting next to an icon, albeit an advertising icon, yes it was Katie, who, in the 1960s, made Oxo a household name.

When I informed her I was writing this book, she encouraged me to persevere. She appeared to agree with my thesis, which was, and still is, the power of advertising has been greatly exaggerated and a book of this nature was needed to counteract the propaganda regarding the effect of advertising upon all of our lives.

Hence this book.

It has come about as a result of literally hundreds and thousands of conversations, emails, letters etc, over the course of, at least 30 years with many, many people. These conversations took place in New York, Sydney, Melbourne, Manila, Los Angles, Chicago, Tokyo, Singapore, London and many, many other cities.

This is not to boast about a much travelled life, but to make the observation that, over the course of 30 years, I have met many intelligent people who worked in marketing or advertising, from all over the world, who were already expressing great concern about the process of marketing and advertising and the direction it was heading.

Most of these people have moved on to other, more 'rewarding' occupations, or have retired.

However, I have to make a special thanks to Laurie Orme who had the patience to read the first draft proofs from, so to speak, cover to cover, and encouraged me to persevere. Then I have to thank Jeff Palfreyman in Washington DC, and now Huntington Beach, California, who did the same from the perspective of his vast and considerable experience in the direct marketing field. Jeff, in my opinion, is one of the best and most knowledgeable people within the wide and diverse field of marketing communication, although I suspect even he has become more than a little jaundiced with the industry. And my thanks to Marc Lewis, whom I bludgeoned into helping me with introductions to possible publishers, and to giving me his advice gained from him already having successfully published one book and is in the course of writing his second.

While we were the pioneers of interactive communication to the marketing and, to a far lesser extent, the advertising community, we have to make space here to thank all those authors who have written their own books on the subject of communications and the future, which I have used in the preparation of this book.

It is impossible to finish a task such as this without realising how lucky I have been in my family and friends. A book such as this grows, not just from a few years of intensive research, but also from a lifetime spent in the company of people who are more than interested in the subject.

Further reading

Bunting, Sandra Cottier, *Advertising*, (Hodder Arnold H&S, September 1996).

Clark, Eric. *The Want Makers*, (Viking Adult, 1989).

Cole, Kris. *Complete Idiot's guide to clear communication*, (Indianapolis, Ind, Alpha, 2002). (Voice inflection, facial movements, body language and word choice all contribute to making a skilled communicator.)

Davis, Martyn. *Effective Use of Advertising Media*, (Random House Business Books, 1988.)

de Bono, Edward. *Simplicity*, (Penguin Books, 1999). (Have you ever given up trying to programme your video recorder or use a feature on your computer because the instructions are so complicated?)

Dimbleby, Richard; Burton, Graeme. *Between Ourselves*, (Hodder Arnold Publication, 2006). (An introduction to interpersonal communication.)

Douglas, Torin. (consulting editor Barry Day), *The complete guide to advertising*, (Papermac, 1987).

Fletcher, Winston. *How to Capture the Advertising High Ground*, (Centuary, 1994). (It's as sure as death and taxes that in Kuwait or Kashmir or Kowloon, even the most carefully controlled multinational plan will run into a local glitch.)

Handy, Charles. *The Age of Unreason*, (Harvard Business School, 2002). (If you put a frog in cold water and slowly heat it, the frog will eventually let itself be boiled to death.)

Clark, Erick. *The Want Makers. Lifting the lid off the World Advertising Industry: How they make you buy*, (Guild, 1988).

Levine, Rick; Locke, Christopher; Searls, Doc; Weinbergerm, David. *The Cluetrain Manifesto*, (Perseus Publishing, 2000). (The end of business as usual. The Cluetrain Manifesto is to marketing and communications what the open-source movement is to software development).

Lewis, David; Bridger, Darren. *The Soul of the New Consumer: Authenticity what we buy and why in the New Economy*, (Nicholas Brealey, 2001). (No more holding people to hostage through 30-second commercials. No more hype. No more ignorant customers. No more local monopolies. No more search costs. No more 'Get into your car and come to us'. If you're paying attention, you're sweating by now.)

Lewis, Michael. *The Future Just Happened*, (Hodder and Stoughton, 2001). (A splendid, entirely satisfying book, intelligent and fun and revealing and troubling in the correct proportions.)

Locke, Christopher. *Gonzo Marketing: Winning through the Worst Practices*, (Perseus Publishing, 2001). (Pink Floyd meets business: over-the-top, infuriating, provocative, entertaining and always stimulating.)

McArthur, C. *From Cuneiform to Computers*, (Oxford University Press, 2002).

McKenna, Regis. *Real Times*, (Harvard Business School Press, 1997). (Regis McKenna never ceases to challenge the conventional wisdom. The notion of eliminating hierarchy and long-term planning and creating real time management that focuses on delivery, results, and customer needs.)

Mirabito, Michael. *The New Communication Technologies*, (Focal Press, 2004).

Morris, Desmond. *Manwatching*, (Abrams, 1977). (A field guide to human behaviour.)

Mountfield, Anna. Looking Back at *Sending Messages*, (Schoolhouse Press, 1990).

Munnelly, Brendan. *Information & Communication*, (Prentice Hall, 2005). (Everything you need to know about communication)

Myers, Gregg. *Ad Worlds: Brands, Media, Audiences*, (Arnold, 1999).

Nicholas, Joe. *Advanced Media Communication & Production*, (Nelson 1998).

Peppers, Don; Rogers, Martha. *The One to One Future*, (Doubleday, 1993). (Unusual insight into how marketers can serve each other and every consumer.)

Peters, Tom. *The Circle of Innovation*, (Random House, 1999). (You can't shrink your way to greatness.)

Peters, Tom; Austin, Nancy. *A Passion for Excellence*, (Random House, 1985). (Dedicated to innovative leaders everywhere, this book is for all concerned about the pursuit of excellence in the business world and in public service.)

Philo, Greg. *Seeing is Believing: The Influence of Television*, (Routledge & Keegan, 1981).

Jonathon Taylor. *Marketing Communications*, (Kogan Page, 1997). (The integrated approach. I recommend the integrated approach to Marketing Communications.)

Solymar, L. *Getting the Message. A History of Communication*, (Oxford University Press, 2009). (Explores the story of communication from Roman times to the present, with the advent of email, the internet and mobile phones. Looks to the future of communication and the implications for our everyday lives.)

Tanaka, Keiko. *Advertising language*, (Routledge, 1999). (A pragmatic approach to advertising in Britain and Japan.)

Watson, James. *Dictionary of Media & Communication Studies*, (Hodder Arnold, 2006.)

Wunderman, Lester. *Being Direct: Making Advertising Pay*, (Direct Marketing Association, 2004). (A must-read for anyone who wants to understand what direct marketing is about.)

Further reading: articles

The Sunday Times. Improve your Communication Skills, (Kogan Page Ltd, September 2006).

DHSS, Getting your Message Across. (DHS Press Release, September 2005).

Financial Times. Communicate to Win, (Kogan Page Ltd, 2000).

Oktober Books

Witness the revolution

Oktober Books is a publishing house, based in the South West of England.

We are interested in publishing edgy writing, somewhere off the mainstream, which gives a voice to those outside the comfortable centre of our society.

Any challenging ideas about contemporary society, or the shape of things to come will fit into our ethos.

www.oktoberbooks.co.uk

Also published by Oktober Books:

The Joy of Ex by Edward Keating

It all starts with a drunken bet, well actually it starts with a lot of Jose Cuervo, some casual sex with strangers and a drunken concept, the drunken bet kind of follows naturally along behind.

Nick is convinced the spark that gets a girl to sleep with him is still there between them forever, however the relationship ends. His best mate Blake doesn't agree. Instead Blake believes the fire between two people is gone, on one side at least, when things come to an end.

To find out who is right Nick bets Blake he cannot seduce and bed six of his ex girlfriends/one nighters – and provide photographic evidence.

So is an ex girlfriend ripe for seduction, or is everything truly over when one partner says goodbye?

Blake is about to find out when he discovers The Joy of Ex.

For further details about The Joy of Ex visit www.thejoyofex.co.uk

While books have no official ratings, Oktober Books recommends this novel is not read by anyone under the age of 18.

To order your copy of The Joy of Ex by Edward Keating
visit www.oktoberbooks.co.uk or write to PO Box 520, Weston-super-Mare, BS23 9EE.

Also published by Oktober Books:

Fragments by Edward Keating

From the author of The Joy of Ex comes a collection of stories covering a wide range of intense and challenging themes.

In the story *Tracey*, 20-something Spence and his mates have discovered a great way of using the internet to make quick cash using the age old industry of exploiting women.

Scanning The Sky explores what would happen if we discovered television signals from another world.

Heiress Nebraska Branning is dubbed Queen of the Damned in an article for a small niche newspaper. Reporter Vanessa Farraday follows up the story for her national magazine and meets *America's Sweetheart*.

To order your copy of Fragments by Edward Keating
visit www.oktoberbooks.co.uk or write to PO Box 520, Weston-super-Mare, BS23 9EE.

Do you want your writing published by Oktober Books?

If you are looking to publish a non-fiction work, or your fiction, either a novel or short story(ies), and you feel your work reflects the edgy ethos behind Oktober Books, please get in touch with us by emailing:

submissions@oktoberbooks.co.uk

Please no attachments, any examples of your work should be included in the body of the email.

Include the first three chapters (fiction or non-fiction), or three short stories and a synopsis of the rest of the work. And a little bit about yourself as well.

life stories
lifestoriesandmemories.co.uk

Give future generations a precious gift they'll treasure - your life story

- Professionally produced by an experienced writer
- Present your story as a book, booklet or in a tasteful commemorative folder
- Include cherished photos
- Store your story online

Web: www.lifestoriesandmemories.co.uk
email: contactus@lifestoriesandmemories.co.uk

Renaissance Communications
bringing communication back to marketing

Communication should be a two-way process. We can make sure you have proper dialogue with your customers. By building a proper relationship through real interaction you can increase sales.

We have a proven and completely accountable technique which will minimise the sales impact of media while allowing you to make spending cuts. Applying our methodology has been the foundation of the tremendous sales growth we have achieved for a range of blue chip companies.

Contact us at:

info@tvtag.co.uk

www.tvtag.co.uk
www.renaissancemarketing.co.uk

EHWLC LEARNING CENTRE
EALING GREEN